T0301949

An Analysis of

Robert D. Putnam's

Bowling Alone
The Collapse and Revival
of American Community

Elizabeth Morrow
with
Lindsay Scorgie-Porter

Published by Macat International Ltd
24:13 Coda Centre, 189 Munster Road, London SW6 6AW.

Distributed exclusively by Routledge
2 Park Square, Milton Park, Abingdon, Oxon OX14 4RN
711 Third Avenue, New York, NY 10017, USA

Routledge is an imprint of the Taylor & Francis Group, an informa business

Copyright © 2017 by Macat International Ltd
Macat International has asserted its right under the Copyright, Designs and Patents Act
1988 to be identified as the copyright holder of this work.

The print publication is protected by copyright. Prior to any prohibited reproduction, storage in
a retrieval system, distribution or transmission in any form or by any means, electronic, mechanical, recording or otherwise, permission should be obtained from the publisher or where
applicable a license permitting restricted copying in the United Kingdom should be obtained
from the Copyright Licensing Agency Ltd, Barnard's Inn, 86 Fetter Lane, London EC4A 1EN, UK.

The ePublication is protected by copyright and must not be copied, reproduced, transferred,
distributed, leased, licensed or publicly performed or used in any way except as specifically
permitted in writing by the publishers, as allowed under the terms and conditions under which
it was purchased, or as strictly permitted by applicable copyright law. Any unauthorised distribution or use of this text may be a direct infringement of the authors and the publishers' rights
and those responsible may be liable in law accordingly.

www.macat.com
info@macat.com

Cataloguing in Publication Data
A catalogue record for this book is available from the British Library.
Library of Congress Cataloguing-in-Publication Data is available upon request.
Cover illustration: Etienne Gilfillan

ISBN 978-1-912303-43-4 (hardback)
ISBN 978-1-912127-72-6 (paperback)
ISBN 978-1-912282-31-9 (e-book)

Notice
The information in this book is designed to orientate readers of the work under analysis,
to elucidate and contextualise its key ideas and themes, and to aid in the development
of critical thinking skills. It is not meant to be used, nor should it be used, as a
substitute for original thinking or in place of original writing or research. References and
notes are provided for informational purposes and their presence does not constitute
endorsement of the information or opinions therein. This book is presented solely for
educational purposes. It is sold on the understanding that the publisher is not engaged
to provide any scholarly advice. The publisher has made every effort to ensure that
this book is accurate and up-to-date, but makes no warranties or representations with
regard to the completeness or reliability of the information it contains. The information
and the opinions provided herein are not guaranteed or warranted to produce particular
results and may not be suitable for students of every ability. The publisher shall not be
liable for any loss, damage or disruption arising from any errors or omissions, or from
the use of this book, including, but not limited to, special, incidental, consequential or
other damages caused, or alleged to have been caused, directly or indirectly, by the
information contained within.

CONTENTS

THE MACAT LIBRARY

The Macat Library is a series of unique academic explorations of seminal works in the humanities and social sciences – books and papers that have had a significant and widely recognised impact on their disciplines. It has been created to serve as much more than just a summary of what lies between the covers of a great book. It illuminates and explores the influences on, ideas of, and impact of that book. Our goal is to offer a learning resource that encourages critical thinking and fosters a better, deeper understanding of important ideas.

Each publication is divided into three Sections: Influences, Ideas, and Impact. Each Section has four Modules. These explore every important facet of the work, and the responses to it.

This Section-Module structure makes a Macat Library book easy to use, but it has another important feature. Because each Macat book is written to the same format, it is possible (and encouraged!) to cross-reference multiple Macat books along the same lines of inquiry or research. This allows the reader to open up interesting interdisciplinary pathways.

To further aid your reading, lists of glossary terms and people mentioned are included at the end of this book (these are indicated by an asterisk [*] throughout) – as well as a list of works cited.

Macat has worked with the University of Cambridge to identify the elements of critical thinking and understand the ways in which six different skills combine to enable effective thinking.
Three allow us to fully understand a problem; three more give us the tools to solve it. Together, these six skills make up the **PACIER** model of critical thinking. They are:

ANALYSIS – understanding how an argument is built
EVALUATION – exploring the strengths and weaknesses of an argument
INTERPRETATION – understanding issues of meaning

CREATIVE THINKING – coming up with new ideas and fresh connections
PROBLEM-SOLVING – producing strong solutions
REASONING – creating strong arguments

To find out more, visit **WWW.MACAT.COM.**

CRITICAL THINKING AND *BOWLING ALONE*

Primary critical thinking skill: INTERPRETATION
Secondary critical thinking skill: REASONING

American political scientist Robert Putnam wasn't the first person to recognize that social capital – the relationships between people that allow communities to function well – is the grease that oils the wheels of society. But by publishing *Bowling Alone*, he moved the debate from one primarily concerned with family and individual relationships one that studied the social capital generated by people's engagement with the civic life. Putnam drew heavily on the critical thinking skill of interpretation in shaping his work. He took fresh looks at the meaning of evidence that other scholars had made too many assumptions about, and was scrupulous in clarifying what his evidence was really saying. He found that strong social capital has the power to boost health, lower unemployment, and improve life in major ways. As such, any decrease in civic engagement could create serious consequences for society. His interpretation of multifarious issues led him to the understanding that if America is to thrive, its citizens must connect.

ABOUT THE AUTHOR OF THE ORIGINAL WORK

Robert D. Putnam was born in the United States in 1941 and grew up in a small Midwestern town where people actively took part in community life. He studied at Yale in the United States and Oxford University in England, before becoming a professional academic, making his name at Harvard. Putnam's unique understanding of the importance of social capital—the civic values that help communities thrive—means US presidents Barack Obama and George W. Bush sought his advice, while President Clinton referenced Putnam's ideas in his 1995 State of the Union address.

ABOUT THE AUTHORS OF THE ANALYSIS

Dr Elizabeth Morrow is currently a research fellow at the Department of Political Science and International Studies, University of Birmingham. She began her career as a lawyer with the Victorian state government in Melbourne before completing her PhD in Politics in the Department of Political Economy at King's College London.

Dr Lindsay Scorgie Porter is Visiting Assistant Professor in Politics at the University of Western Ontario. She holds a PhD in politics and international studies from the University of Cambridge and an MSc in global politics from the London School of Economics.

ABOUT MACAT

GREAT WORKS FOR CRITICAL THINKING

Macat is focused on making the ideas of the world's great thinkers accessible and comprehensible to everybody, everywhere, in ways that promote the development of enhanced critical thinking skills.

It works with leading academics from the world's top universities to produce new analyses that focus on the ideas and the impact of the most influential works ever written across a wide variety of academic disciplines. Each of the works that sit at the heart of its growing library is an enduring example of great thinking. But by setting them in context – and looking at the influences that shaped their authors, as well as the responses they provoked – Macat encourages readers to look at these classics and game-changers with fresh eyes. Readers learn to think, engage and challenge their ideas, rather than simply accepting them.

'Macat offers an amazing first-of-its-kind tool for interdisciplinary learning and research. Its focus on works that transformed their disciplines and its rigorous approach, drawing on the world's leading experts and educational institutions, opens up a world-class education to anyone.'

Andreas Schleicher
Director for Education and Skills, Organisation for Economic
Co-operation and Development

'Macat is taking on some of the major challenges in university education … They have drawn together a strong team of active academics who are producing teaching materials that are novel in the breadth of their approach.'

Prof Lord Broers,
former Vice-Chancellor of the University of Cambridge

'The Macat vision is exceptionally exciting. It focuses upon new modes of learning which analyse and explain seminal texts which have profoundly influenced world thinking and so social and economic development. It promotes the kind of critical thinking which is essential for any society and economy. This is the learning of the future.'

Rt Hon Charles Clarke, former UK Secretary of State for Education

'The Macat analyses provide immediate access to the critical conversation surrounding the books that have shaped their respective discipline, which will make them an invaluable resource to all of those, students and teachers, working in the field.'

Professor William Tronzo, University of California at San Diego

WAYS IN TO THE TEXT

KEY POINTS

- The American academic Robert D. Putnam was born in 1941 and grew up in Ohio. His experience of small-town life there may have helped him develop his theories on social capital.*

- Putnam's approach in *Bowling Alone* was unique because he saw social capital not in terms of interactions between individuals, as previous sociologists had done, but in terms of an individual's engagement with civic life.

- *Bowling Alone* remains one of the most frequently cited works of social science. Not only has it found an audience in many areas, including politics and academia, but it has also attracted interest from the wider public.

Who Is Robert D. Putnam?

Born in 1941, Robert D. Putnam grew up in a small Midwestern town in the United States. His parents—a schoolteacher and a builder—were moderate Republicans who both participated actively in civic life. Speaking of his hometown, Port Clinton, Ohio, Putnam said, "I was really blessed in growing up in a place that had a lot of social capital."*[1] It is possible that the models of civic engagement* (the ways of working to make a difference to the quality of life in a community) that Putnam experienced during his formative years sparked his interest in the subject, which forms the major theme of *Bowling Alone*.

Putnam left his small town for the suburbs of Philadelphia, receiving his undergraduate degree from Swarthmore College. He won a Fulbright Scholarship to study at Oxford University and received both his master's and doctorate from Yale. He began his career as a professional academic at the University of Michigan, moving to Harvard University in 1979. Here, in addition to his teaching duties, Putnam also served as dean of Harvard's John F. Kennedy* School of Government. He wrote *Bowling Alone* during his tenure at Harvard, publishing it first as an article in the quarterly academic publication *Journal of Democracy*[*2] and then expanding it to book length.

Raised as a Christian in the Methodist Church,* Putnam converted to Judaism* when he married his wife, Rosemary, in 1963. He has said that part of his attraction to the religion is the "unique and intense community" he sees in Jewish life.[3]

What Does *Bowling Alone* Say?

Robert D. Putnam writes in his book *Bowling Alone: The Collapse and Revival of American Community*, published in 2000, that his "aim is to promote (and perhaps contribute to) a period of national deliberation and experimentation about how we can renew American civic engagement and social connectedness in the twenty-first century."[4] The work documents the decline of civic engagement in the United States and the consequent reduction in social capital.

Social capital has long been recognized as the grease that oils the wheels of society. It facilitates trust, creates bonds among neighbors, even helps boost employment. Putnam defines it as the "connections among individuals—social networks and the norms of reciprocity [give and take] and trustworthiness that arise from them."[5]

Putnam did not invent the notion of social capital, but he did treat it in a novel way. Other sociologists had applied the concept to individuals' interactions with each other. But Putnam's work introduces a conceptual twist: instead of looking for social capital in the context of individuals and groups, he takes a broader view, examining the social capital generated by people's engagement with the civic life of their towns or cities.[6]

Putnam analyzed various measures—volunteering, attendance at town meetings, membership of formal organizations, and even the throwing of informal dinner parties—to demonstrate that levels of engagement have fallen since the end of World War II.* In the same time frame, Americans' distrust of their government increased.

In Putnam's view, the sport of bowling exemplifies this theme perfectly: while the number of people who go bowling has increased in the past two decades, the number participating in bowling leagues* has decreased. "Bowling alone" may provide exercise, but it does not afford any outlet for social interaction or the kinds of civic discussions that can occur in groups.

Having established the framework of civic disengagement, Putnam turns to a core question of his book: who—or what—should take responsibility for the decline in social capital in the United States? Like a detective sifting through the evidence, Putnam considers a list of suspects. He notes that pressures of time and money, the disintegration of the family unit, and the rise of mass media and television have all contributed to the reduction of social capital. But the real culprit, he decides, is change over generations.

Putnam's novel analysis struck a chord with readers. In his view, the storm that his ideas provoked demonstrated that he "had unwittingly articulated an unease that had already begun to form in the minds of ordinary Americans."[7]

Putnam's research has spurred other academics to explore the impact of social capital on civic life. And by writing in plain, accessible English, Putnam opened up the discussion of civic disengagement to a wide population of readers and thinkers.

Why Does *Bowling Alone* Matter?

It would be difficult to overstate the impact of *Bowling Alone*, which has become one of the most frequently cited social science publications of the past half-century. Putnam's ideas have been applied to a variety of social challenges, ranging from health debates to the resolution of disputes. His advice has been sought by political leaders of all stripes— from current US president Barack Obama* to former president George W. Bush*; from former British prime minister Gordon Brown* to Libyan dictator Muammar Gadaffi.* President Bill Clinton* even referenced Putnam's ideas in his 1995 State of the Union address.*

Putnam's book persuaded the academic community that social capital was indeed in decline. This reset the starting point in the debate over social capital. And so, rather than arguing about whether social capital *was* declining, academics moved on to consider the *reasons behind* this decline. Putnam contended that generational change had fueled America's civic disengagement. Not everyone agreed with this analysis and some began to search for other explanations.

More recently, researchers influenced by Putnam have employed his concept of social capital, and his research methods, to better understand problems outside those discussed in *Bowling Alone*, including immigration, health care, and even the civic life of other countries.

Putnam's work continues through the Saguaro Seminar,* an initiative he founded in 1995 at Harvard University's John F. Kennedy School of Government. Its website says the Saguaro Seminar's mission is to "improve social capital measurement and data and to investigate ways to build social capital in a changing world across several domains."[8]

A decade and a half after its publication, *Bowling Alone* remains essential reading for anyone interested in social capital and civic engagement.

NOTES

1   C-SPAN Booknotes, "Robert Putnam: Bowling Alone," *C-SPAN Booknotes* (December 24, 2000), http://www.booknotes.org/FullPage. aspx?SID=159499-1, accessed February 19, 2015.

2   Robert D. Putnam, "Bowling Alone: America's Declining Social Capital," *Journal of Democracy* 6, no. 1 (1995): 65–78.

3   Mark K. Smith, "Robert Putnam," *The Encyclopaedia of Informal Education*, http://www.infed.org/thinkers/putnam.htm, accessed February 19, 2015.

4   Robert D. Putnam, *Bowling Alone: The Collapse and Revival of American Community* (New York: Simon & Schuster, 2000), 28.

5   Putnam, *Bowling Alone*, 19.

6   Alejandro Portes, "Social Capital: Its Origins and Applications in Modern Sociology," *Annual Review of Sociology* 24 (1998): 18–19.

7   Putnam, *Bowling Alone*, 506.

8   Harvard Kennedy School, "The Saguaro Seminar," http://www.hks.harvard. edu/programs/saguaro/, accessed February 20, 2015,.

SECTION 1
INFLUENCES

MODULE 1
THE AUTHOR AND THE
HISTORICAL CONTEXT

KEY POINTS

- Bowling Alone is one of the most cited social publications of the past 50 years.

- Putnam's childhood in Port Clinton, Ohio, exposed him to lots of different models of civic engagement.*

- By the 1990s, many people—including not only Putnam, but also President Bill Clinton*—found it increasingly apparent that America's social bonds were weakening.

Why Read This Text?

In the 2000 best seller Bowling Alone: The Collapse and Revival of American Community, Robert D. Putnam—Malkin Professor of Public Policy at Harvard University's John F. Kennedy* School of Government—charts the rise and fall of civic engagement in the United States. Putnam's work focuses on the importance of social capital*—the connections between individuals, and the social networks, trust, and reciprocity (give and take) that such connections involve.[1]

According to Putnam, social networks foster a generalized reciprocity, best summed up as, "I'll do this for you without expecting anything specific back from you, in the confident expectation that someone else will do something for me down the road."[2]

Bowling Alone became a best seller in the US and has since gained wide international importance. Its impact has been enormous—indeed, it was one of the most repeatedly cited social science publications of the past 50 years. The ideas in the text have been

> ❝ I was really blessed in growing up in a place that had a lot of social capital. ❞
>
> Robert D. Putnam, *C-SPAN Booknotes*

applied to various social issues, including health dialogues and settling disputes. Putnam's definition of social capital and his method of quantitative analysis have been used by subsequent studies of social capital and community disengagement.

Author's Life

Putnam is the child of a schoolteacher mother and a builder father, both of whom were moderate Republicans and active in civic life. He describes his parents as great examples of the "long civic generation."[3] The small town where he grew up—Port Clinton, Ohio—he characterizes as an area high in social capital, where people trusted and looked after each other.[4] Being raised in a place where the benefits of civic engagement were apparent clearly had a lasting effect on Putnam, planting the seeds of an idea that became the central theme of Bowling Alone.

Putnam received his undergraduate degree from the prestigious Swarthmore College in the suburbs of Philadelphia and completed his postgraduate education at the universities of Oxford and Yale. Around the time of his marriage to Rosemary in 1963, Putnam converted to Judaism,* his wife's religion. He has spoken about how he was drawn to the "unique and intense community" of the religion.[5] While Bowling Alone is not a religiously inspired text, it is possible that the strong civic culture shared in Jewish communities may have furthered Putnam's interest in the topic.

Putnam wrote Bowling Alone during his tenure at Harvard University, where he has taught since 1979. Some of the examples of civic participation in the book focus on his personal experiences in his New England neighborhood. Before working at Harvard, Putnam taught at the University of Michigan.

Author's Background

Throughout Bowling Alone, Putnam says that social capital in the US is declining as civic engagement wanes: Americans are less likely to vote, volunteer their time, attend church, and even have friends over for dinner. In fact, during the early 1990s, voter turnout had declined by nearly a quarter from the level it had been at in the 1960s. Attendance at public meetings had also plummeted in the previous two decades and the number of volunteers in organizations such as the Boy Scouts of America* and the Red Cross* had also gone down.[6] So, in a broad sense, the text comes out of the post-World War II* American experience of a gradual decline in civic engagement since the 1960s.

In the 1990s this issue finally began to gain a significant amount of attention. In his 1995 State of the Union* address, President Bill Clinton lamented the fraying of community bonds. Like Putnam, Clinton noted the drop in attendance at Parent Teacher Association* gatherings, town hall meetings, and at the places where children played sport. Clinton said, "The great strength of America ... has always been our ability to associate with people who were different from ourselves and to work together to find common ground."[7]

NOTES

1   Robert D. Putnam, Bowling Alone: The Collapse and Revival of American Community (New York: Simon & Schuster, 2000), 19.

2   Putnam, Bowling Alone, 21.

3   The American Interest, "Bowling with Robert Putnam," The American Interest 3, no. 3 (2008), http://www.the-american-interest. com/2008/01/01/bowling-with-robert-putnam/, accessed February 19, 2015.

4   The American Interest, "Bowling with Robert Putnam."

5   Mark K. Smith, "Robert Putnam," The Encyclopaedia of Informal Education, http://www.infed.org/thinkers/putnam.htm, accessed February 19, 2015.

6   Robert D. Putnam, "Bowling Alone: America's Declining Social Capital," Journal of Democracy 6, no. 1 (1995): 65–78.

7   William J. Clinton, "State of the Union Address (January 24, 1995)," in Weekly Compilation of Presitdential Documents, ed. National Archives.

MODULE 2
ACADEMIC CONTEXT

KEY POINTS

- Civic engagement* has always been of great interest in the discipline of politics.

- Nineteenth-century historian Alexis de Tocqueville* may be considered the "forefather" of the concept of social capital,* although that particular term was not used until 1916 when it was introduced by L. J. Hanifan.*

- Like his academic predecessors, Putnam considers social capital in a positive light. But unlike prior academics, he focuses specifically on social capital at the town/city level.

The Work In Its Context

Robert D. Putnam, author of *Bowling Alone: The Collapse and Revival of American Community*, did not create the concept of social capital. As he acknowledges, the term "turns out to have been independently invented at least six times over the twentieth century, each time to call attention to the ways in which our lives are made more productive by social ties."[2]

The discipline of politics has always concerned itself with the wider subject of civic engagement—on a national or a community level. In fact, the first use of the phrase "social capital" occurred *not* in an academic context, but in a governmental one.

In a 1916 handbook for teachers, a supervisor of rural schools in West Virginia named L. J. Hanifan argued that successful schools relied on community involvement.[3] Hanifan believed that people are more likely to get involved when doing so adds to their social capital: "… those tangible substances [that] count for most in the daily lives of

❝ The term social capital itself turns out to have been independently invented at least six times over the twentieth century, each time to call attention to the ways in which our lives are made more productive by social ties. ❞

Robert D. Putnam, *Bowling Alone*

people: namely good will, fellowship, sympathy, and social intercourse among the individuals and families who make up a social unit."[4] But Hanifan's new term attracted little attention and the phrase largely disappeared for decades, to be intermittently "rediscovered" at various points during the second half of the twentieth century.[5]

Overview of the Field

Robert Putnam frequently and favorably cites the nineteenth-century French historian and political thinker Alexis de Tocqueville throughout *Bowling Alone*. Tocqueville is best known for his text *Democracy in America*. Published in two volumes in 1835 and 1840, it presents a study of America's egalitarian ideals and flourishing democratic system. Putnam describes Tocqueville as being the "patron saint of contemporary social capitalists"[6] because of the light he shines on the civic life of the US, which at the time was still a very young country. Or, as modern cultural sociologist and ethnographer* Paul Lichterman* puts it, "Tocqueville still is the most prominent single theoretical muse for social capital."[7]

Tocqueville praises America's active civic life, noting the frequency with which Americans attend meetings to discuss and debate a range of issues. This level of civic engagement, Tocqueville believed, encouraged a transparent democratic system, which in turn gave citizens more incentive to participate in the process, further strengthening the democracy. Or, in Tocqueville's words, "Feelings and ideas are renewed, the heart enlarged, and the understanding developed only by the reciprocal action of men one upon another."[8] Tocqueville's work is clearly a cultural forerunner of *Bowling Alone*.

Academic Influences

More recently, a number of influential authors have also advanced the concept of social capital. Economist Glenn Loury* believed the concept could help explain how social positioning impacts employment opportunities. Social theorist Pierre Bourdieu* focused on the social and economic resources embedded in social networks. Sociologist James Coleman* argued that social capital helps with productive activity because a group with high levels of trust among its members can accomplish more than a group lacking that trust.[9] Putnam follows the trend established by his academic predecessors, viewing high stocks of social capital as generally beneficial— facilitating trust, creating employment opportunities, and providing economic value.

But Putnam puts forward a novel conceptual approach in his work. Rather than seeking social capital in the context of individuals and groups, he assumes a more expansive viewpoint, looking at the social capital produced by people's participation in civic life in their towns or cities.[10]

Like many of the authors who have written about social capital— including Hanifan, Loury, and Coleman—Putnam is an American and his work focuses on the American experience. He draws all of his data from the United States, and several of the community organizations he focuses on, such as marching bands, the Parent Teacher Association, and the Elks* social club, are uniquely American.

NOTES

1   Robert D. Putnam, *Bowling Alone: The Collapse and Revival of American Community* (New York: Simon & Schuster, 2000), 19.

2   Putnam, *Bowling Alone*, 19.

3   Putnam, *Bowling Alone*, 19.

4   Putnam, *Bowling Alone*, 19.

5   Putnam, *Bowling Alone*, 19.

6   Putnam, *Bowling Alone*, 292.

7   Paul Lichterman, "Social Capital or Group Style? Rescuing Tocqueville's Insights on Civic Engagement," *Theory and Society* 35, no. 5–6 (2006): 534.

8   Alexis de Tocqueville, *Democracy in America* (Garden City, NY: Doubleday, 1969), 515.

9   Glenn C. Loury, "A Dynamic Theory of Racial Income Differences," in *Women, Minorities and Employment Discrimination*, ed. Phyllis A. Wallace and Annette M. LaMond (Lexington, MA: Lexington Books, l977); Pierre Bourdieu, "The Forms of Capital," in *Handbook of Theory and Research for the Sociology of Education*, ed. John G. Richardson (Westport, CT: Greenwood Publishing Group, 1986); James S. Coleman, "Social Capital in the Creation of Human Capital," *American Journal of Sociology* 94 (1988): 95–120.

10 Alejandro Portes, "Social Capital: Its Origins and Applications in Modern Sociology," *Annual Review of Sociology* 24 (1998): 18–19.

MODULE 3
THE PROBLEM

KEY POINTS

- Putnam's text launches four separate inquiries: Has social capital* in the United States declined? If so, why? Does it matter? What can be done to rebuild social capital?

- At the time when Putnam was writing, most people argued that social capital was a highly beneficial and necessary component of community, with limited negative side effects.

- Putnam largely built upon the arguments and assumptions of the mainstream debate, but he was the first to expand the notion of social capital from the individual to the civic level.

Core Question

Five years before Robert D. Putnam published *Bowling Alone: The Collapse and Revival of American Community*, he wrote an article in the quarterly academic publication *Journal of Democracy** titled "Bowling Alone: America's Declining Social Capital."[1] In the article, Putnam pointed to the declining membership of friendly fraternal organizations and the Parent Teacher Association as evidence that Americans were becoming increasingly disengaged from their communities.[2] The article generated a great deal of publicity—initially complimentary, but later critical, with one headline claiming, "Bowling Alone is Bunk."[3] The critics' central argument was that by looking only at established, formal organizations, Putnam had overlooked the connections that may be formed by participating in new groups, or by an ad hoc, or more informal, involvement in civic life.[4]

There was some truth in these negative views, as even Putnam

> ❝ A society characterized by generalized reciprocity [give and take] is more efficient than a distrustful society, for the same reason that money is more efficient than barter. If we don't have to balance every exchange instantly, we can get a lot more accomplished. Trustworthiness lubricates social life. Frequent interaction among a diverse set of people tends to produce a norm of generalized reciprocity. ❞
>
> Robert D. Putnam, *Bowling Alone*

acknowledged. The claims in his 1995 article rested on slender evidence and he later admitted he had relied on flawed data, due to a calculating error.[5] When he set out to amend and expand the article into the book-length study *Bowling Alone*, he broadened his research to include newer organizations and gatherings as informal as private dinner parties.

- He wanted the book to answer four questions:
- Is civic engagement in America indeed declining?
- If so, what began this trend?
- What ramifications does it have for society?
- What can be done to rebuild social capital?

The Participants

When Putnam wrote *Bowling Alone*, social scientists generally agreed that social capital was a positive—and highly important—phenomenon. The French sociologist Pierre Bourdieu,* for example, characterized it as the profits that amass from group membership. James Coleman,* an American sociologist, suggested that a densely populated community will have a large amount of social capital, which will facilitate trust among its members and make the community more productive. The economist Glenn Loury* believed that social capital could help explain how social positioning impacts employment opportunities. Finally, sociologist Mark Granovetter* argued that a person with a broad social network would have a better chance of finding out about employment opportunities.[6]

Occasionally, one of these researchers hinted that social capital could also have a downside. For instance, in his widely cited article "Social Capital in the Creation of Human Capital," Coleman recognized that social capital had the potential to be harmful. For instance, people within a group might show a lack of tolerance to people outside. Yet he still focused almost exclusively on its benefits.[7]

The Contemporary Debate

Putnam acknowledged that the writers who explored social capital before him had done a great deal of important research: "Much of my argument—and indeed, much of this book—involved simply integrating masses of relevant research that had already been honed by experts in a dozen separate fields over several decades."[8] Indeed, Putnam references his predecessors' and contemporaries' ideas throughout *Bowling Alone*.

Putnam's argument that social capital creates safe and productive neighborhoods recalls Coleman's belief that social capital encourages high levels of trust within a community.[9] Coleman had earlier presented this argument in an article that focused on the mostly Jewish wholesale diamond market of New York, whose traders intermarry, live in the same community in the Brooklyn area of the city, and attend the same synagogues. When negotiating a sale, one diamond trader will often hand over a bag of stones to another merchant for inspection. They do this without putting in place any formal insurance arrangements and the merchant receiving the goods could easily steal the gems or substitute inferior stones for the merchandise received. But such deceit does not seem to occur, largely because the merchants are tied through family, community, and religious affiliation. If a merchant were caught stealing or cheating, he would risk severing all those ties.[10]

Similarly, Putnam's discussion of economic prosperity—which suggests that the right social networks can help individuals get ahead—were points earlier made by Loury and Granovetter, who respectively argued that black people have trouble getting jobs because of their parents' typically low socioeconomic status, and that individuals with wider social networks will acquire information relevant to job hunting more easily.[11]

Bowling Alone also arguably conforms to Coleman's pattern of admitting that social capital has potentially harmful effects but focuses overall on its upside. Putnam dedicates 65 pages of *Bowling Alone* to the benefits of social capital. As he sees it, they range from better health and education outcomes to greater economic productivity and democratic participation. He devotes only 13 pages to a discussion of the possible disadvantages of social capital, including solidarity within the group to the exclusion of others, or antagonism and intolerance toward people who are outside of the group.

Putnam departs from his predecessors in the way he broadens the concept of social capital. Previous analyses tended to focus on the relationship of an individual with his or her social network. In *Bowling Alone*, Putnam discusses social capital in terms of the level of civic engagement displayed in America's towns and cities.[12] His bigger-picture analysis of social capital represented a fresh research approach.

NOTES

1   Robert D. Putnam, "Bowling Alone: America's Declining Social Capital," *Journal of Democracy* 6, no. 1 (1995): 65–78.

2   Putnam, "Bowling Alone: America's Declining Social Capital."

3   Robert D. Putnam, *Bowling Alone: The Collapse and Revival of American Community* (New York: Simon & Schuster, 2000), 506–7.

4   Putnam, *Bowling Alone*, 508.

5   Putnam, *Bowling Alone*, 507–8.

6   Pierre Bourdieu, "The Forms of Capital," in *Handbook of Theory and Research for the Sociology of Education*, ed. John G. Richardson (Westport, CT: Greenwood Publishing Group, 1986); James S. Coleman, "Social Capital in the Creation of Human Capital," *American Journal of Sociology* 94 (1988): 95–120; Mark S. Granovetter, "The Strength of Weak Ties," *American Journal of Sociology* 78, no. 6 (1973), 1360–80.

7   Coleman, "Social Capital in the Creation of Human Capital."

8   Putnam, *Bowling Alone*, 507.

9   Putnam, *Bowling Alone*.

10 Coleman, "Social Capital in the Creation of Human Capital."

11 Glenn C. Loury, "A Dynamic Theory of Racial Income Differences," in *Women, Minorities and Employment Discrimination*, ed. Phyllis A. Wallace and Annette M. LaMond (Lexington, MA: Lexington Books, l977); Granovetter, "The Strength of Weak Ties."

12 Alejandro Portes, "Social Capital: Its Origins and Applications in Modern Sociology," *Annual Review of Sociology* 24 (1998): 18.

MODULE 4
THE AUTHOR'S CONTRIBUTION

KEY POINTS

- Putnam's primary aim in *Bowling Alone* is to promote awareness of the decline of social capital* in the United States. He wants to spark debate and incite experimentation to reverse this trend.

- The author's comprehensive argument about the level of civic engagement in America's towns and cities—and the data behind this argument—broke new ground in the subfield of social capital.

- *Bowling Alone* incorporated and built upon previous work done on social capital and civic engagement, but in many ways it remains a novel text.

Author's Aims

Robert D. Putnam begins *Bowling Alone: The Collapse and Revival of American Community* by establishing that Americans have become increasingly disengaged from civic life since the end of World War II.* They volunteer less, vote less frequently, attend church less often, and even throw fewer dinner parties for their friends.

After establishing the problem by analyzing these trends, Putnam examines the causes and consequences of weakening social bonds. He also discusses what Americans can do to reverse the trend of disengagement.

The concepts of social capital and civic disengagement did not originate with *Bowling Alone*. The novelty lies in Putnam's comprehensive argument that community engagement was declining in the US and his identification of the reasons for this decline. While previous analyses of social capital had mainly focused on the

❝ [My] aim is to promote (and perhaps contribute to) a period of national deliberation and experimentation about how we can renew American civic engagement* and social connectedness in the twenty-first century. **❞**

Robert D. Putnam, *Bowling Alone*

relationship of an individual with his or her social network, Putnam looked at social capital generated by civic engagement within America's towns and cities.[1]

Approach

Putnam sticks quite rigidly to his analysis of civic disengagement. Recognizing the risk that nostalgia about past levels of civic engagement may distort the facts, Putnam decided "to count things."[2] He does indeed delve into the facts and figures relevant to civic participation, such as newspaper readership, hours spent volunteering, and dinner parties hosted. Similarly, Putnam presents quantifiable statistics relating to the beneficial effects of social capital in many aspects of our lives, such as health, education, and the economy. Perhaps in a deliberate attempt to promote continued civic connectedness and help rebuild social capital, Putnam directs readers to two websites with which he is affiliated—www.bowlingalone.com and www.bettertogether.org.

To an extent, Putnam's inquiries about social capital in America resemble his 1993 work on the importance of social capital for democracy in Italy. That 20-year study focused on government and civic engagement in various regions of Italy. However, once Putnam turned his attention to the decline in social capital in the United States—perhaps because it was an area he knew well, being his home country—he broke new ground. In "Bowling Alone" he focuses on the impact of civic engagement on the performance of government, as well as on the outcomes for health, economics, and education. He stated, "The norms and networks of civic engagement also powerfully affect the performance of representative government."[3]

Contribution In Context

Putnam was not the first person to articulate the concept of social capital. That honor belongs to L. J. Hanifan.* A state supervisor of rural schools in West Virginia in 1916, Hanifan noted, "The individual is helpless socially, if left to himself. If he comes into contact with his neighbor, and they with other neighbors, there will be an accumulation of social capital, which may immediately satisfy his social needs and which may bear a social potentiality sufficient to the substantial improvement of living conditions in the whole community."[4]

To an important extent, Putnam can be seen as continuing the intellectual trend begun by Hanifan and taken up by later authors such as Glenn Loury,* Pierre Bourdieu,* Mark Granovetter,* and James Coleman.* Putnam drew on their arguments and similarly recognized that social capital can help create employment opportunities, foster trust, and provide economic value. However, Putnam diverged from previous intellectual trends in the field of social capital in several important ways. First, because he equated social capital not with individual interactions but with the interactions between citizens and the towns and cities in which they live. Second, because he made a comprehensive argument that the American community was in trouble. And, finally, because he attempted to identify the reasons for the worrisome decline in social engagement.

NOTES

1   Alejandro Portes, "Social Capital: Its Origins and Applications in Modern Sociology," *Annual Review of Sociology* 24 (1998): 18.

2   Robert D. Putnam, *Bowling Alone: The Collapse and Revival of American Community* (New York: Simon & Schuster, 2000), 26.

3   Robert D. Putnam, "Bowling Alone: America's Declining Social Capital," *Journal of Democracy* 6, no. 1 (1995): 2.

4   Putnam, *Bowling Alone*, 19.

SECTION 2
IDEAS

MODULE 5
MAIN IDEAS

KEY POINTS

- Putnam discusses four key themes throughout *Bowling Alone*: social change in the US; the value of social networks; the factor(s) responsible for the decline in social capital;* and, finally, the potential for renewal and regeneration of community.

- The main argument of the text is that Americans need to start rebuilding their social capital—they need to begin reconnecting with each other.

- Putnam has been praised for making *Bowling Alone*'s key ideas very accessible.

Key Themes

From the outset, Putnam argues that Americans have changed the ways in which they relate to each other and to the institutions of their common civic life. These changes have led to more disengagement, which means less social capital. He writes that "we Americans need to reconnect with each other. That is the simple argument of this book."[2]

Social networks have value, in Putnam's view, and social contacts—whether they arise from participation in formal organizations or from informal interactions—have a positive impact on the productivity of individuals and groups.[3]

He also clearly demonstrates the negative results of civic disengagement. To understand how Americans can reverse this trend and reconnect with each other, he looks into the reasons why they have become less engaged.

❝ [W]e Americans need to reconnect with each other.
That is the simple argument of this book. **❞**

Robert D. Putnam, *Bowling Alone*

Exploring The Ideas

Putnam investigates the themes of social change in America and the
value of social networks repeatedly and in a variety of ways throughout
Bowling Alone. He sets the stage with a series of stories about declining
civic engagement in the United States: the closing of a bridge club,
school marching band uniforms that go unused due to low interest in
the activity, a defunct knitting league. One of these anecdotes inspired
the title of the book: Putnam found that people were bowling on their
own, doing without the camaraderie of the traditional league format.
Putnam highlights one member of a local bowing league in Michigan
who donated a kidney to a fellow bowler.[4] If they hadn't been
involved in the league, the men would never have met. As Putnam
concludes, the fact that "they bowled together made all the
difference."[5]

Putnam then moves from the anecdotal (views based on personal
accounts) to the empirical (views based on evidence). To do this he
uses statistics, graphs, and pie charts to point out the decline in civic
engagement* in political, religious, philanthropic (acting to promote
the good of others), and social groups.

Having established the framework of civic disengagement, Putnam
then introduces a core question of his book: who—or what—should
take responsibility for America's declining social capital? Like a
detective sifting through the evidence, Putnam assesses a list of varied
suspects. He considers constraints on time and money, the
fragmentation of the family unit, and the increasing importance of
mass media and television as all playing a part in the reduction of social
capital. It's worth noting that Putnam was writing before the

smartphone was everywhere, or he surely would have added the Internet to this list. But the real culprit, he decides, is what he calls generational change.

People born before World War II* were unusually civic-minded. Putnam suggests that the heightened sense of civic obligation in wartime—from both those in uniform and those on the home front—helped foster social solidarity and shaped an entire generation of people. These people were prepared to "ask not what your country can do for you—ask what you can do for your country,"[6] in the stirring words of President John F. Kennedy's* 1961 inaugural address. "By 1965 disrespect for public life, so endemic in our history, seemed to be waning," Putnam observes.[7] More parents wanted their children to go into politics than ever before; more people trusted their neighbors.

This, however, has not been the case for subsequent generations.[8] Putnam suggests that the decline in civic engagement began when the Baby Boomers*—the nickname for Americans born after World War II,* a period that saw a significant increase in the birth rate—began to come of age, in the late 1960s.

The final theme of *Bowling Alone* is renewal and regeneration: how Americans can create social capital and once again engage with their communities. Putnam outlines a variety of solutions to civic ills, ranging from youth participation in well-designed service-learning programs* (where people learn skills while doing work that benefits the community) to the introduction of electronic communication and entertainment that will reinforce community engagement.

Language And Expression

Bowling Alone is a highly accessible work. Reviewers have praised the book for its readability, clear arguments, and unpretentious prose. Perhaps because of this accessibility, the book became a national best seller. For more analytical readers, *Bowling Alone* also contains detailed appendices setting out the data Putnam relied on to build his arguments. Putnam claims to have included them to convince skeptical readers, but the majority of the information would likely remain unintelligible to readers outside of the academic world.[9]

If anything, Putnam's aims were perhaps too sweeping. While he dedicates over 100 pages to tracking down the "culprit" behind America's civic disengagement, the solution he presents is little more than an afterthought, discussed in 12 pages toward the end of the book.

Arguing for reconnection, Putnam claims he wants to contribute to the national discussion about renewing civic engagement. But he does not offer any comprehensive or substantial answers to readers who themselves want to encourage more Americans to engage with their communities.

NOTES

1   Robert D. Putnam, *Bowling Alone: The Collapse and Revival of American Community* (New York: Simon & Schuster, 2000), 19.

2   Putnam, *Bowling Alone*, 28.

3   Putnam, *Bowling Alone*, 19.

4   Putnam, *Bowling Alone*, 28.

5   Putnam, *Bowling Alone*, 28.

6   John F. Kennedy, Inaugural Address (January 20, 1961), http://www.ushistory.org/documents/ask-not.htm, accessed 17 March, 2015.

7   Putnam, *Bowling Alone*, 17.

8   Putnam, *Bowling Alone*, 247–77.

9   Putnam, *Bowling Alone*, 26.

MODULE 6
SECONDARY IDEAS

KEY POINTS

- One of the main secondary ideas in *Bowling Alone* is the distinction between bridging* and bonding* social capital.*

- Because of a lack of reliable nationwide data, Putnam does not strongly emphasize the difference between these two types of social capital.

- Putnam also engages in a brief, underdeveloped discussion of whether the entry of women into the paid workforce has had an impact on the decline in civic engagement.*

Other Ideas

An important secondary idea in Robert D. Putnam's *Bowling Alone: The Collapse and Revival of American Community* is the distinction between bridging and bonding social capital. As Putnam explains, "Of all the dimensions along which forms of social capital vary, perhaps the most important is the distinction between bridging (or inclusive) and bonding (or exclusive)."[1]

According to Putnam, bridging social capital looks outward and encompasses people from a broad social spectrum.[2] The Civil Rights Movement,* youth service groups, and religious organizations are examples of bridging social capital.[3] Bonding social capital, in contrast, is likely to be inward-looking and to reinforce "exclusive identities and homogenous groups."[4] Bonding social capital derives from organizations such as those affiliated with a particular ethnic group, church-based reading groups, or elite country clubs.[5]

Bonding and bridging social capital serve different ends, but both

ff The movement of women out of the home and into the paid workforce is the most portentous social change of the last half century. ""

Robert D. Putnam, *Bowling Alone*

can be useful. Putnam notes that, "Bonding social capital is good for undergirding specific reciprocity [give and take] and mobilizing solidarity."[6] The tight network of an ethnic area, for instance, can provide social and psychological support to its members. It may even help with financing a market and providing reliable labor for local entrepreneurs.[7] In contrast, bridging social capital helps to circulate information and provide links to external assets.[8] Although bonding social capital may create strong in-group loyalty, it may also create out-group antagonism, or hostility, and even foster anti-liberal tendencies.[9]

Exploring The Ideas

Putnam acknowledges that because he was unable to find "reliable, comprehensive, nationwide measures of social capital that neatly distinguish 'bridgingness' and 'bondingness'," he has chosen not to differentiate the two types in *Bowling Alone*.[10] So the reader cannot know whether the social capital he writes of is created by bonding (which Putnam, like others, recognizes can promote illiberal tendencies) or bridging, which most authors seem to recognize as a force for good.

In an academic context, a distinction between bridging and bonding social capital would provide a conceptual framework through which we might identify the potential benefits and pitfalls of each type of social capital. However, lacking the relevant data, Putnam has made the wise decision not to distinguish between the two types of social capital in *Bowling Alone*.

The distinction that Putnam does draw between bridging and

bonding social capital could be a product of his own understanding of the changing nature of social capital. Putnam has admitted that when he was writing his 1995 article, he believed that social capital would always have a beneficial impact on society. Later, he recognized that some social networks could, in fact, be detrimental to society.[11]

Overlooked

One argument Putnam makes in *Bowling Alone* seems both underdeveloped and overlooked. In the third section of the book he lists factors that may be responsible for the greatly diminished level of civic engagement in America. Buried in a subsection called "Pressures of Time and Money" is the idea that the entry of women into the workforce—which Putnam calls "the most portentous [that is, important and serious] social change of the last half century"[12]—may have contributed to civic disengagement.

By engaging in unpaid community activities such as volunteering with the Parent Teacher Association,* stay-at-home mothers contributed significantly to America's social capital. But when women entered the paid workforce they no longer had the leisure time to be as heavily involved in such activities. Crucially, men did not pick up the civic slack.

Putnam acknowledges that paid employment significantly reduces civic involvement: Full-time work reduces female volunteering by 50 percent.[13] Yet despite such data, he concludes that women's participation in the workforce did not severely weaken civic engagement. He notes that between 1965 and 1985, even stay-at-home mothers reduced their civic participation.[14] In Putnam's view, women entering the workforce may account for no more than 10 percent of the responsibility for civic decline. In contrast, he believes the effects of television to be 25 percent responsible.[15]

Little academic attention has been paid to this point, though it has gained some traction in the popular media. Margaret Talbot,* a staff writer for *The New Yorker* magazine, questioned Putnam's conclusion. She argued that women's participation in the workforce must be more relevant to the decline of social capital than Putnam suggests. Talbot wrote that "women have traditionally been more avid social capitalists then men and now have much less free time to exercise that avidity."[16] She proposed that this aspect of *Bowling Alone* has remained underexplored because "Television viewing certainly makes a more politically palatable target than women's paid labor. Not many of us leap to the defense of couch potato-ism as a civic virtue, whereas quite a few of us defend the expansion of autonomy and opportunity for women."[17]

Rather than suggesting that we rush to restore the level of civic engagement that we had in the past, Talbot notes, "It may be that with women in the paid labor force, we will never enjoy quite the level of associational life we had in the 1950s. And in the end that trade-off may be worth it."[18]

KEY QUESTIONS

Synthesize: What are the different types of social capital, and how can these be differentiated?

Analyze: How does the distinction between the two different kinds of social capital aid our understanding of civic engagement in America?

Apply: Do you believe that women entering the workforce had as relatively small an impact on the level of social capital in America as Putnam purports?

NOTES

1   Robert D. Putnam, *Bowling Alone: The Collapse and Revival of American Community* (New York: Simon & Schuster, 2000), 22.

2   Putnam, *Bowling Alone*, 22.

3   Putnam, *Bowling Alone*, 22.

4   Putnam, *Bowling Alone*, 22.

5   Putnam, *Bowling Alone*, 22.

6   Putnam, *Bowling Alone*, 22.

7   Putnam, *Bowling Alone*, 22.

8   Putnam, *Bowling Alone*, 22.

9   Putnam, *Bowling Alone*, 23, 358.

10   Putnam, *Bowling Alone*, 23–4.

11   *The American Interest*, "Bowling with Robert Putnam," *The American Interest* 3, no. 3 (2008), http://www.the-american-interest.com/2008/01/01/bowling-with-robert-putnam/, accessed February 19, 2015.

12   Putnam, *Bowling Alone*, 194.

13   Putnam, *Bowling Alone*, 194.

14   Putnam, *Bowling Alone*, 196, 203.

15   Putnam, *Bowling Alone*, 283.

16   Margaret Talbot, "Who Wants to Be a Legionnare?" *New York Times* , June 25, 2000, http://www.nytimes.com/books/00/06/25/reviews/000625.25talbott.html, accessed February 19, 2015.

17   Talbot, "Who Wants to Be a Legionnare?".

18   Talbot, "Who Wants to Be a Legionnare?".

MODULE 7
ACHIEVEMENT

KEY POINTS

- Putnam's *Bowling Alone* struck a chord with readers in general, while also inspiring academics and influencing American policy-makers.

- The author's previously published article on a very similar subject helped encourage interest in the book and probably contributed to its positive reception.

- While some of Putnam's findings may apply in other cultural and political contexts, the main limitation of *Bowling Alone* is its unwaveringly American focus.

Assessing The Argument

In *Bowling Alone: The Collapse and Revival of American Community*, Robert D. Putnam articulates his concern that social capital has been declining as civic disengagement has been rising in America. The concepts of social capital* and civic disengagement are not new, but his novel analysis resonated with readers. As Putnam admits, the storm his ideas provoked showed that he "had unwittingly articulated an unease that had already begun to form in the minds of ordinary Americans."[1]

Making use of previously unanalyzed data from a study over a number of years by a large advertising agency, the DDB Needham Life Style Survey* on the social habits of Americans, Putnam documented an unprecedented level of civic disengagement. By shedding light on new data, Putnam's research likely helped other academics interested in the lifestyles of Americans. And by writing in plain, accessible English, Putnam opened up the discussion to a wide population

> ❝ The picture in the UK is not as dramatic as that
> painted by US academic Robert Putnam. Informal
> social networks, membership of community
> organisations and voluntary groups appear to have held
> up relatively well ... ❞
>
> Ben Rogers and Emily Robinson, *The Benefits of Community Engagement:*
> *A Review of the Evidence*

of thinkers.

The concepts in *Bowling Alone* inspired part of President Bill Clinton's* 1995 State of the Union address,* provoking a national debate about the state of American society.[2] Leaders in other disciplines have also looked to *Bowling Alone* to see how an increase in engagement might help solve some of society's problems. In the field of medicine, for example, thought leaders have looked at the impact social capital can have on health outcomes, with studies linking good social capital to success in lowering binge drinking and smoking, among other benefits.[3]

Achievement In Context

In 1995, five years before publishing the book *Bowling Alone*, Putnam wrote an article on the same subject. That article—also called "Bowling Alone" (only the subtitles of the book and the article differ)—attracted a wide readership, which greatly influenced the book's reception and ultimate success.

Putnam has acknowledged that his 1995 article hit home with Americans who had witnessed their bowling alleys and socially oriented Elks* clubs close for lack of patrons. Those Americans had also seen their once-frequent dinner parties and card games become more sporadic.[4] Younger Americans are increasingly uninterested in activities like these. But Putnam's observations on community life would chime particularly with Americans old enough to remember a different civic culture in the United States.

When he turned the article into a book-length study, Putnam added more examples of community involvement. He focused the majority of them on activities that recalled an earlier era: the bridge club, bowling leagues,* and sewing and knitting circles. These were not activities in which younger people took part. So Putnam clearly knew the demographics of the people who had read and cited his "Bowling Alone" article.

Putnam has acknowledged that the general public and an academic audience may have different concerns around social capital. In an email written to a friend before the book's publication, Putnam suggested that academics were more interested in seeing *evidence* that social capital was actually declining. The general population, on the other hand, was already *convinced* of the decline and wanted to know what could be done to reverse the trend.[5] The fact that his book has sections devoted to proving the decline of social capital, as well as suggestions about how to strengthen American civic engagement, indicates that Putnam sought to satisfy both audiences—and he succeeded. *Bowling Alone* has become both a best seller and one of the most cited social science publications of the past 50 years.[6]

Limitations

As the full title, *Bowling Alone: The Collapse and Revival of American Community*, suggests, Putnam's book focuses on the experience of social capital and civic engagement within the United States. Some of the examples of civic participation he refers to—league bowling, membership of the Elks club, attendance at a Veterans of Foreign Wars* gathering—are unique to, or at least originated in, the United States. However, it is possible to draw parallels. In a country such as the United Kingdom, for instance, readers may be able to equate bowling with darts, while Australian readers may liken the Veterans of Foreign

Wars club to their own country's defense force support organization, the Returned and Services League.

Nevertheless, a UK government report noted that while social scientists and politicians have become concerned with community disengagement, "The picture in the UK is not as dramatic as that painted by US academic Robert Putnam. Informal social networks, membership of community organisations and voluntary groups appear to have held up relatively well …"[7] While this is not a critique of Putnam's text as such, it helps to illuminate one limitation of the book: its analysis is less relevant in a country whose social capital and civic engagement trends do not closely resemble America's. For example, Japan, Sweden, and the Netherlands have actually seen their levels of social capital increase slightly.[8] Finally, some of the arguments that Putnam makes are irrelevant in certain cultural and/or political contexts. His discussion about the importance of social capital for democracy, for example, would be irrelevant in a country that has an autocratic* ruler with uncontrolled power.

NOTES

1   Robert D. Putnam, *Bowling Alone: The Collapse and Revival of American Community* (New York: Simon & Schuster, 2000), 506.

2   Alejandro Portes, "Social Capital: Its Origins and Applications in Modern Sociology," *Annual Review of Sociology* 24 (1998): 19.

3   Simon Szreter and Michael Woolcock, "Health by Association? Social Capital, Social Theory, and the Political Economy of Public Health," *International Journal of Epidemiology* 33, no. 4 (2004): 651.

4   Thomas H. Sander and Robert D. Putnam, "Still Bowling Alone?: The Post-9/11 Split," *Journal of Democracy* 21, no. 1 (2010): 9–16.

5   Putnam, *Bowling Alone*, 509.

6   Harvard University Department of Government, "Robert Putnam," Department of Government, Harvard University, http://www.gov.harvard.edu/people/faculty/robert-putnam, accessed February 19, 2015.

7   Ben Rogers and Emily Robinson, *The Benefits of Community Engagement: A Review of the Evidence* (London: Home Office Active Citizenship Centre, 2004), 11.

8   David Halpern, *Social Capital* (Cambridge: Polity Press, 2005).

PLACE IN THE AUTHOR'S WORK

KEY POINTS

- Putnam's chief focus throughout his life's work has been civic engagement* and social capital.*

- Although it was not his first great success (or his last), *Bowling Alone* remains a milestone in Putnam's career.

- His two best-known, most highly regarded works are *Bowling Alone* and the 1993 book *Making Democracy Work.*

Positioning

By the time *Bowling Alone: The Collapse and Revival of American Community* was published in 2000, Robert D. Putnam was already one of America's leading social scientists. He held a professorship at Harvard University, and had served as dean of its prestigious John F. Kennedy* School of Government. His previous book, 1993's *Making Democracy Work*, had been very well received. Yet despite these achievements, *Bowling Alone* marked a milestone in Putnam's career. It became a national best seller and is one of the most cited social science publications of the past half-century, alongside *Making Democracy Work*.

Putnam has a long-standing interest in the concept of social capital. *Making Democracy Work* examined the impact that civic engagement has on good government.[1] The 20-year study, which focused on government and civic engagement in various regions of Italy, concluded, "The norms and networks of civic engagement also powerfully affect the performance of representative government."[2] In *Bowling Alone*, Putnam returns to the idea that civic engagement is important for good government. But in this later work he expands his inquiry considerably. He considers whether civic engagement in

> **❝[Making Democracy Work is] a classic in political science.❞**
> New York Times Book Review

America has actually declined, why it has declined, and what can be done to encourage Americans to become more engaged.

Putnam still retains his interest in America's social capital. In 2003 he published *Better Together: Restoring the American Community* with co-author Lewis Feldstein.* *Better Together* focused on "exceptional cases in which creative social entrepreneurs [are] moving against the nationwide tide and creating vibrant new forms of social connectedness."[3] From 2003 to 2008, Putnam was involved in a major five-year study that explored the impact of social diversity on social capital. Putnam concluded—somewhat controversially—that increased immigration and social diversity reduces trust, solidarity, and social capital.[4]

Integration

Putnam's body of work can certainly be considered coherent and unified. Nevertheless, there are slight variations in each of his works on social capital.

While *Making Democracy Work* focused on social capital and civic engagement, it argued that social capital is likely to be fostered by participation in horizontal networks,* not vertical networks.* A horizontal network brings together groups of equal status and power and includes neighborhood associations, choral societies, and sports clubs.[5] In contrast, vertical networks link unequal groups in a relationship of hierarchy and dependence.[6] Examples of vertical networks include the Mafia.* The social capital benefits in a horizontal network are unlikely to be found in a vertical network, because such relationships cannot sustain social trust and cooperation.[7] Despite the overlap in research interests between *Making Democracy Work* and *Bowling Alone*, Putnam does not consider the distinction between horizontal and vertical networks in the latter's discussion of social capital.

Putnam's 1995 article "Bowling Alone: America's Declining Social Capital" is in many ways a blueprint for the book, touching on many of the themes he expanded on in the later work. However, while the article created something of a sensation, it also generated a backlash. *Washington Post* columnist Robert Samuelson* and political science professor Everett Carll Ladd* criticized Putnam for not considering that civic engagement may take different forms.[8] For instance, while people no longer bowl in leagues, youth football has become more popular. Putnam appears to explicitly address these criticisms in the book, expanding his reach to less formal forms of engagement and providing a wealth of empirical proof (based on factual evidence) to convince his "show me" readers.[9]

Significance

Putnam's body of work has been highly influential in academic circles—a quick look at the number of times his work has been cited confirms this. He has helped steer academic research of social capital, and the arguments made in *Bowling Alone* have been tested in other countries such as Germany and Slovenia. While Putnam has now written 14 books, there is no doubt that *Bowling Alone* and *Making Democracy Work* are the more important texts in terms of establishing his academic reputation.

Putnam's influence also extends beyond academia and into the political arena. The "Bowling Alone" article inspired passages of President Bill Clinton's* 1995 State of the Union address,* and politicians across a broad political spectrum—from President George W. Bush* to Vice President Al Gore* in the US, from British prime minister Gordon Brown* to Libyan dictator Muammar Gaddafi*—

have spoken to Putnam about his work.[10] Indeed, on several occasions Putnam has urged the American government to improve its understanding of the state of America's social capital. It is little wonder that the *Sunday Times* in Britain called Robert Putnam "the most influential academic in the world today."

NOTES

1   Robert D. Putnam, Robert Leonardi, and Raffaella Nanetti, *Making Democracy Work: Civic Traditions in Modern Italy* (Princeton, NJ: Princeton University Press, 1994).

2   Robert D. Putnam, "Bowling Alone: America's Declining Social Capital," *Journal of Democracy* 6, no. 1 (1995): 2.

3   Robert D. Putnam and Lewis Feldstein, *Better Together: Restoring the American Community* (New York: Simon & Schuster, 2004), x.

4   Harvard Kennedy School Insight, "Robert Putnam on Immigration and Social Cohesion" (February 11, 2008), http://www.hks.harvard.edu/news-events/publications/insight/democratic/robert-putnam, accessed June 7, 2013.

5   Putnam, Leonardi, and Nanetti, *Making Democracy Work*, 173.

6   Putnam, Leonardi, and Nanetti, *Making Democracy* Work, 173.

7   Putnam, Leonardi, and Nanetti, *Making Democracy Work*, 175.

8   Everett C. Ladd, "The Data Just Don't Show Erosion of America's 'Social Capital'," *The Public Perspective* (June/July 1996); Robert J. Samuelson, "'Bowling Alone' is Bunk," *Washington Post*, April 10, 1996.

9   Robert D. Putnam, *Bowling Alone: The Collapse and Revival of American Community* (New York: Simon & Schuster, 2000), 26.

10 Madeleine Bunting, "Capital Ideas," *The Guardian*, July 18, 2007, http://www.guardian.co.uk/society/2007/jul/18/communities.guardiansocietysupplement, accessed February 19, 2015; Louis Uchitelle, "Lonely Bowlers, Unite: Mend the Social Fabric; A Political Scientist Renews His Alarm at the Erosion of Community Ties," *New York Times*, May 6, 2000, http://www.nytimes.com/2000/05/06/arts/lonely-bowlers-unite-mend-social-fabric-political-scientist-renews-his-alarm.html?pagewanted=all&src=pm, accessed June 7, 2013.

SECTION 3
IMPACT

MODULE 9
THE FIRST RESPONSES

KEY POINTS

- There were four main criticisms of Putnam's 1995 "Bowling Alone" article, many of which were also applied to the book that followed: that he employed circular logic;* that he ignored various social trends; that he assumed involvement in an association to be necessarily positive; and that he placed too much emphasis on the responsibility of the individual to remedy the decline in America's social capital.*

- The 2000 book *Bowling Alone* can largely be seen as an acceptance of, and response to, these criticisms.

- In expanding the argument, Putnam employed more empirical (evidence-based) data to support his arguments, which largely convinced the former skeptics.

Criticism

While Robert D. Putnam's *Bowling Alone: The Collapse and Revival of American Community* became a national best seller and attracted glowing reviews in major US newspapers and other publications, the book received a mixed reception in academic circles. Putnam's critics generally came from academic backgrounds themselves, strongly suggesting that the debate around his work stems from intellectual differences. There were four main criticisms, as outlined below.

First, critics said that Putnam employed circular logic—where a person begins by assuming the truth of the argument's end point, without providing evidence to back up the conclusion. Alejandro Portes,* chair of the Department of Sociology at Princeton University, suggests that Putnam's argument makes social capital both a cause and

> ❝[Lessons] of trust and solidarity, of developing an 'I' into a 'we', do not strengthen democracy when the trust, solidarity, and the 'we' are such that they do not go beyond the group in question. ❞
>
> Simone Chambers and Jeffrey Kopstein, "Bad Civil Society"

an effect:[1] social capital creates outcomes that benefit a community, such as economic development. And if a community has those outcomes, Putnam infers that it also has social capital.[2] While Portes leveled his original criticisms at Putnam's 1995 article, the book-length study suffers from the same problem. Further, the book makes claims such as, "For North Carolina to see educational outcomes similar to Connecticut's ... residents could do any of the following ... double their frequency of club meeting attendance ... or attend church two more times per month."[3] Putnam presents these statistical formulas even as he admits that he has not established what causes what.[4]

Second, Putnam has been criticized for ignoring, or quickly dismissing, social trends that run counter to his argument. For instance, American sociologist Robert Wuthnow* claims that while some forms of social capital have declined, society has evolved newer ways of connecting with friends and neighbors, such as volunteering.[5] Feminist scholars argue that Putnam relies too heavily on formal acts of participation, such as voting, while ignoring the more informal forms of participation and connectedness that women traditionally prefer.[6]

Throughout *Bowling Alone*, Putnam argues that participation in clubs and voluntary associations strengthens democracy by teaching people how to debate issues with civility, among other things. But Canadian sociologists Simone Chambers* and Jeffrey Kopstein* dispute Putnam's assumption that civic participation will produce the sort of social capital that will enhance, rather than weaken, democracy.[7] Chambers and Kopstein coined the term "bad civil society," noting that involvement with an association may not always be a positive thing. After all, the Mafia* is an association, as is the white supremacist* group the Ku Klux Klan.*[8]

Perhaps most importantly, Putnam's critics say he has placed too much responsibility for remedying America's civic disengagement on the individual, and not enough on government.[9] This criticism is of particular importance, because it could influence debate in both academic and policy-making circles about how to rebuild social capital.

Responses

Many ideas that Robert Putnam explores in *Bowling Alone* appeared five years earlier in his article "Bowling Alone: America's Declining Social Capital."[10] This article received a huge amount of publicity and was followed by a critical backlash. Putnam accepted and responded to many of those criticisms as he was writing his book.

One of the harshest critics was the political scientist Everett Carll Ladd,* who cited an increase in charitable contributions to argue that civic engagement in America had actually increased since the 1960s.[11] Putnam squarely addresses Ladd's counterargument in *Bowling Alone*, observing that while the sheer number of contributions may have increased, the total amount of these gifts has shrunk as a percentage of the country's total income.

And does writing a check generate social capital? Putnam thinks not. He argues that while membership in community organizations has increased, most members have no personal involvement with the organizations they nominally belong to—they merely make donations. In expanding the "Bowling Alone" article into his book, Putnam relied on additional data taken from the membership lists of various community organizations and data from the DDB Needham Life

Style Survey,* a study undertaken by a large advertising agency that ran over many years. This data demonstrated that active involvement—measured by the number of people attending meetings and holding leadership positions—has fallen dramatically.

Conflict And Consensus

Putnam's detractors made some good points and he acknowledged as much, wondering whether he had overstated his case in the article. Perhaps the trends in community participation had not fallen as much as he had actually thought.[12] In fact, Putnam has since admitted that the claims in his 1995 article were based upon rather slim evidence, and the following year he also realized he had relied on flawed data.[13] In the book, Putnam attempts to silence his critics by using empirical evidence to show sweeping trends of civic disengagement that have not been remedied by community involvement in a non-traditional area. The most valuable tool at his disposal, Putnam notes, was the DDB Needham Life Style Study.

To a large extent, Putnam's revisions in the *Bowling Alone* book appeared to convince skeptics. One critic acknowledged that while many of the claims in Putnam's article had been cast in doubt, "by adding in large, new data-sets and squeezing them dry, Putnam not only salvaged his argument, he gained the high ground."[14]

NOTES

1   Alejandro Portes, "Social Capital: Its Origins and Applications in Modern Sociology," *Annual Review of Sociology* 24 (1998): 19.

2   Portes, "Social Capital," 19.

3   Robert D. Putnam, *Bowling Alone: The Collapse and Revival of American Community* (New York: Simon & Schuster, 2000), 301.

4   Putnam, *Bowling Alone*, 334.

5   Robert Wuthnow, "United States: Bridging the Privileged and the Marginalized?," in *Democracies in Flux: The Evolution of Social Capital in Contemporary Society*, ed. Robert D. Putnam (New York: Oxford University Press, 2002), 60.

6   Dietlind Stolle and Marc Hooghe, "Inaccurate, Exceptional, One-Sided or Irrelevant? The Debate About the Alleged Decline of Social Capital and Civic Engagement in Western Societies," *British Journal of Political Science* 35, no. 01 (2005): 154.

7   Simone Chambers and Jeffrey Kopstein, "Bad Civil Society," *Political Theory* 29, no. 6 (2001): 838.

8   Chambers and Kopstein, "Bad Civil Society," 838.

9   William Maloney, Graham Smith, and Gerry Stoker, "Social Capital and Urban Governance: Adding a More Contextualized 'Top-Down' Perspective," *Political Studies* 48, no. 4 (2000): 802–20.

10 Robert D. Putnam, "Bowling Alone: America's Declining Social Capital," *Journal of Democracy* 6, no. 1 (1995): 65–78.

11 Alan Wolfe, "Bowling with Others," *New York Times*, October 17, 1999, http://www.nytimes.com/books/99/10/17/reviews/991017.17wolfet.html, accessed February 20, 2015.

12 C-SPAN Booknotes, "Robert Putnam: Bowling Alone," *C-SPAN Booknotes* (December 24, 2000), http://www.booknotes.org/FullPage. aspx?SID=159499-1, accessed February 19, 2015.

13 Putnam, *Bowling Alone*, 507–8.

14 Claude S. Fischer, "Bowling Alone: What's the Score?," *Social Networks* 27, no. 2 (2005): 155–67.

MODULE 10
THE EVOLVING DEBATE

KEY POINTS

- Putnam's argument that social capital* was declining in America was largely accepted. This shifted the debate to *why* it was falling.

- While not a "school of thought" per se, in the area of social capital research, people often refer to a "Putnam school" approach.

- Putnam's findings in *Bowling Alone* have been applied to a diverse range of fields and geographic areas—proving that the text has relevance beyond the arena of political science in the United States.

Uses And Problems

Robert D. Putnam's *Bowling Alone: The Collapse and Revival of American Community* persuaded the academic community that social capital was indeed in decline. This reset the starting point for social capital debates. Rather than arguing about *whether* social capital was declining, academics moved on to consider the *reasons behind* this decline. Putnam suggested that generational change had fueled America's civic disengagement. Not everyone agreed with this analysis and some began to search for other explanations.

Similarly, some challenged the solutions Putnam suggested for increasing America's stock of social capital. The book *Social Capital: Critical Perspectives on Community and "Bowling Alone"* collects essays all of which "credit Putnam with effectively demonstrating that American civic life has dramatically changed since the 1950s." Yet it questions other aspects of his thesis.[1] One essay argues that Putnam's work does

> ❝ Since 2000, the Seminar's mission has been to both improve social capital measurement and data and to investigate ways to build social capital in a changing world across several domains. ❞
>
> Harvard Kennedy School, "The Saguaro Seminar"

not adequately appreciate how economic forces can cause civic disengagement. Another says that Putnam too easily dismisses the possibilities of electronic communication to generate social capital.

Schools Of Thought

Bowling Alone remains one of the most frequently cited social science publications of the past 50 years. There is no shortage of writers, academics, and thinkers who identify with, and have been influenced by, the book.

Because Putnam's text is relatively recent, it has not created a comprehensive new school of thought. However, within the area of social capital research, some academics refer to the "Putnam school" approach. Essentially, the school consists of scholars who accept Putnam's definition of social capital, and try to reproduce the quantitative research* methods (using statistical or mathematical data) Putnam employed to measure various aspects of social capital.[2] Quantitative research generally collects data through tests or surveys and should be capable of being replicated—meaning the same type of study can be reproduced many times.[3]

Disciples of the Putnam school, such as Laura Morales,* who studies social capital and immigration, and Dutch academic Peter Geurts,* have employed his concept of social capital and his research methods to better understand problems that are not raised in *Bowling Alone*. While Putnam's text focuses on social capital in the United States, Putnam school sociologists have applied its ideas to Eastern

European states and other countries.

More recently, the Putnam school has turned its attention to the impact of ethnic diversity on social capital. In part, Putnam himself has spearheaded this line of inquiry. But other devotees, including Dutch sociologist Maurice Gesthuizen,* have undertaken quantitative research that focuses on the impact of immigration in nations as diverse as Cyprus, Luxembourg, Malta, and England.[4]

In Current Scholarship

The most faithful, and arguably the most influential, disciples of *Bowling Alone* and its ideas are the staff of the Saguaro Seminar,* an initiative founded by Putnam in 1995 at Harvard University's John F. Kennedy* School of Government in Cambridge, Massachusetts. The saguaro cactus plant, which grows in American deserts, plays a diverse role that allows it to make its ecosystem a better place: birds nest in it, vines grow on its branches, and Native Americans have lived off its fruit. Putnam sees the saguaro as the plant embodiment of the social capital concept.

Unsurprisingly, the Saguaro Seminar essentially mirrors the ideas and beliefs expressed by Putnam in *Bowling Alone*. For example, its website explains that social capital is important because communities with higher levels have better health and education outcomes, as well as less crime and violence.[5] Like *Bowling Alone*, the Saguaro Seminar website attributes the fall in social capital to factors such as urban sprawl, increased television watching, and generational changes in behavior.[6] A section of the website designed to answer frequently asked questions about social capital draws repeatedly on Putnam's research.

The Saguaro Seminar has been of significant political influence within America. The organization has successfully lobbied the US government to measure social capital in its Current Population Survey.[7] In 1997, before he became president of the United States,

Barack Obama* attended some Saguaro Seminar workshops. After his election in 2008 he appointed former Saguaro Seminar staff to senior positions in the White House, where he draws on ideas and skills he learned about during the workshops.[8]

NOTES

1   Scott L. McLean, David A. Schultz, and Manfred B. Steger, eds, *Social Capital: Critical Perspectives on Community and "Bowling Alone"* (New York: New York University Press, 2002), 11.

2   Jonathan Grix, "Introducing Students to the Generic Terminology of Social Research," *Politics* 22, no. 3 (2002): 181.

3   John W. Creswell, *Research Design: Qualitative, Quantitative, and Mixed Methods Approaches* (Thousand Oaks, CA: Sage Publications, 2008), 149.

4   See, for instance, Maurice Gesthuizen, Tom Van Der Meer, and Peer Scheepers, "Ethnic Diversity and Social Capital in Europe: Tests of Putnam's Thesis in European Countries," *Scandinavian Political Studies* 32, no. 2 (2009): 121–42. While this study refutes Putnam's conclusions, it does utilize aspects of his definition of social capital and quantitative methods to test the impact that ethnic diversity has on social capital.

5   Harvard Kennedy School, "The Saguaro Seminar," http://www.hks.harvard.edu/programs/saguaro/, accessed February 20, 2015.

6   Harvard Kennedy School, "The Saguaro Seminar."

7   Social Capital Blog in participation with the Saguaro Seminar, "Advances in Social Capital Measurement," https://socialcapital.wordpress.com/2008/08/07/advances-in-social-capital-measurement/, accessed March 18, 2015.

8   Daniel Burke, "Saguaro Seminar Stays with Obama," *Christianity Today*, June 12, 2009, http://www.christianitytoday.com/ct/2009/juneweb-only/123.55.0.html?start=19, accessed February 19, 2015.

MODULE 11
IMPACT AND INFLUENCE TODAY

KEY POINTS

- Fifteen years have passed since the release of *Bowling Alone*, yet it remains a key text for anyone interested in social capital* and civic engagement.*

- The work challenges the role of electronic communication in developing social capital and the potential harmful effects that involvement with certain associations might have on democracy.

- The book's findings have been applied to the field of health science, where the reception has been generally positive, even if some skepticism exists.

Position

Some 15 years after the publication of Robert D. Putnam's *Bowling Alone: The Collapse and Revival of American Community*, the book is still an important read for anyone interested in social capital and civic engagement. This suggests that, despite the objections raised when the ideas first appeared in a 1995 article, the academic community regards Putnam's work favorably.

One area of ongoing debate concerns the issue of involvement in associations and whether this may promote a type of social capital that is harmful to democracy. Throughout *Bowling Alone*, Putnam argues that participation in clubs and voluntary associations strengthens democracy, because members learn how to debate issues in a polite and civil way. But authors such as the Canadian sociologists Simone Chambers* and Jeffrey Kopstein* have argued that Putnam too readily assumes that civic engagement will benefit democracy.[1] This

" Social capital has been vaunted as the next big idea in social policy and health. "
Kwame McKenzie, Rob Whitly, and Scott Weich, "Social Capital and Mental Health"

discussion comprises part of a wider discourse on the benefits and potential downsides of social capital.

When Putnam published the book in 2000, the Internet had not yet assumed the dominant place it occupies in our lives today. Still, Putnam's text has become part of the debate about the role of electronic communication in developing social capital.

Bowling Alone does contain some observations about the benefits and pitfalls of electronic communication. Putnam recognizes that the anonymity provided by the Internet has the potential to foster discussions in which every participant is on an equal footing. But he argues that it also inhibits interpersonal collaboration and trust by removing the helpful social cues we get from face-to-face interactions.[2] Moreover, while Putnam says that the Internet can help people mobilize politically, he also suggests that the single-issue focus of many Internet-based groups can reduce social cohesion by giving rise to a kind of virtual sameness.[3] Recent studies have speculated that the Internet might increase political participation in countries where there is political apathy and declining voter turnout. Here, the Internet may serve as an alternative to traditional voluntary and civic associations, promoting a convenient and efficient form of sociability.[4]

Interaction

Bowling Alone is still relevant to a broad range of social problems. References to the book appear frequently in contexts ranging from community building to the settlement of disputes to health care.

Putnam's text has had extensive—and rather unexpected—

applications, particularly in the field of health sciences. Putnam touches on the health benefits of social capital in a 10-page section of the book and this relatively brief discussion caught the eye of Richard Wilkinson,* a researcher who compares disease processes between animal and human populations. Wilkinson first applied Putnam's idea of social capital to the field of public health in his book *Unhealthy Societies*.[5] Today, a vast amount of research exists on the role social capital plays in health outcomes. Studies have linked social capital to improvements in child development, lower susceptibility to binge drinking, and sustained participation in anti-smoking programs.[6] Research into the link between social capital and mental health noted that "social capital has been vaunted as the next big idea in social policy and health." Some studies suggest that high levels of social capital also lead to improved mental health outcomes.[7]

The Continuing Debate

Public health researchers have applied the concept of social capital in much the same way as their colleagues have done in the social sciences. Academics generally seem to accept that social capital has benefits. But some skepticism still remains over what the works that purport to show a link between good health and social capital *really* demonstrate. Critics say the health outcomes in such research may depend on their context and may not be broadly applicable.[8] Furthermore, some authors have argued that social capital may actually have negative impacts on health—for instance, people who spend time with an unhealthy circle of friends may form unhealthy habits themselves.[9]

The solutions Putnam puts forward in *Bowling Alone* continue to present a challenge to academics and researchers. Putnam claims that giving young people a civic education can restore social capital. So he sets out a challenge for "America's parents, educators, and, above all, America's young adults" to make sure that within the next decade young people coming of age will be as engaged with their community as their grandparents were at the same age.[10] He issues similar challenges to America's clergy and theologians to encourage religious participation, and to media moguls and journalists to promote electronic communication that reinforces community.[11] Only right at the end of Putnam's discussion about restoring social capital does he challenge government, calling on administrators and politicians to find ways to make sure that more Americans participate in public life.[12] While Putnam places little emphasis on the role of government in creating social capital, some authors, such as city planning expert Mildred Warner* and British academic William Maloney,* have claimed that government policies are critical to promoting the social capital that allows for community development.[13]

NOTES

1   Simone Chambers and Jeffrey Kopstein, "Bad Civil Society," *Political Theory* 29, no. 6 (2001).

2   Robert D. Putnam, *Bowling Alone: The Collapse and Revival of American Community* (New York: Simon & Schuster, 2000), 172–6.

3   Putnam, *Bowling Alone*, 173, 178.

4   See Marko M. Skoric, Deborah Ying, and Ying Ng, "Bowling Online, Not Alone: Online Social Capital and Political Participation in Singapore," *Journal of Computer-Mediated Communication* 14, no. 2 (2009); Caroline J. Tolbert and Ramona S. Mcneal, "Unraveling the Effects of the Internet on Politcal Participation?" *Political Research Quarterley* 56, no. 2 (2003): 175–85.

5   Simon Szreter and Michael Woolcock, "Health by Association? Social Capital, Social Theory, and the Political Economy of Public Health," *International Journal of Epidemiology* 33, no. 4 (2004): 651.

6   Szreter and Woolcock, "Health by Association?," 651.

7   Kwame McKenzie, Rob Whitly, and Scott Weich, "Social Capital and Mental Health," *British Journal of Psychiatry* 181, no. 4 (2002): 280.

8   Szreter and Woolcock, "Health by Association?," 651.

9   Szreter and Woolcock, "Health by Association?," 651.

10 Putnam, *Bowling Alone*, 404.

11 Putnam, *Bowling Alone*, 409–10.

12 Putnam, *Bowling Alone*, 412.

13 Mildred Warner, "Building Social Capital: The Role of Local Government," *Journal of Socio-Economics* 30, no. 2 (2001): 187–92; William Maloney, Graham Smith, and Gerry Stoker, "Social Capital and Urban Governance: Adding a More Contextualized 'Top-Down' Perspective," *Political Studies* 48, no. 4 (2000).

MODULE 12
WHERE NEXT?

KEY POINTS

- While it is likely that *Bowling Alone* will continue to be very relevant, if the United States experienced an upswing in civic participation, then its arguments might come to seem dated.

- In the future, the text will probably have an impact on big debates about immigration and electronic communication. In fact, these debates have already begun with regard to the Internet.

- *Bowling Alone* remains one of the most cited social works of the past half-century and has been credited with stimulating academic debate over social capital* and civic engagement.*

Potential

It seems likely that Robert D. Putnam's *Bowling Alone: The Collapse and Revival of American Community* will always have a place among the most influential social science publications. Students of social capital will continue to find it a "must-read." Indeed, even 15 years after its publication, the work not only continues to be relevant, but is also being applied to new social problems.

If an upswing in civic participation actually did happen, however, then *Bowling Alone* may become less relevant. After the 9/11 attacks* of 2001, Putnam co-published an article suggesting the tragedy had increased civic engagement.[1] However, this increased engagement happened only in certain sections of the US population, namely, the white upper classes. As the article stated, "If the United States is to

> ❝ Public audiences almost never ask whether [civic disengagement] is true, because it rings true to their own experience. ❞
>
> Robert D. Putnam, *Bowling Alone*

avoid becoming two nations, it must find ways to expand the post-9/11 resurgence of civic and social engagement beyond the ranks of affluent young white people."[2] If such an expansion occurred, Putnam's work would probably remain as useful a tool in interpreting the causes of civic *engagement* as it has been in interpreting the current state of *disengagement*.

Future Directions

Some researchers are already beginning to apply Putnam's ideas about social capital and civic disengagement to the issue of immigration. In 2007, seven years after he published *Bowling Alone*, Putnam announced the controversial conclusion that, in the short term, ethnic diversity reduces social capital.[3] National identity never remains static and voters often talk about immigration as one of their top concerns, so we can expect that in the years to come even more researchers will study the impact of immigration on social capital.

Analysts of the influence of the Internet—electronic communications and online social networks—may also apply the ideas Putnam put forward in *Bowling Alone*. Putnam writes briefly about the role of the Internet, but future researchers will want to study in much greater detail how electronic media impact the fabric of our society.

Finally, the most faithful—and arguably most influential—of Putnam's disciples, the staff of the Saguaro Seminar,* will carry on and advance the core messages of *Bowling Alone*. The Saguaro Seminar has already had great political influence in America—for example, through its successful lobbying of the US government to measure social capital in its nationwide surveys. The group will no doubt continue to be influential in the future.

Summary

Bowling Alone swiftly became a best seller in the United States and it has since gained international recognition. As one of the most repeatedly referenced social publications of the past 50 years, it has had a profound impact. *Bowling Alone* has been credited with greatly stimulating—and in fact advancing—academic debate about social capital and civic engagement.

Previous studies of social capital generally focused on an individual and his or her interaction with a group. In *Bowling Alone*, Putnam broadened the discussion to examine social capital in terms of the level of civic engagement in America's towns and cities. His national analysis of social capital had astonishing breadth and showed a novel research approach. He was also the first academic to incorporate data from the DDB Needham Life Style Survey*—a set of data assembled by a large advertising firm over a number of years—into his research.

The reach, appeal, and success of *Bowling Alone* went far beyond academic circles. Putnam felt the book had real impact because he "had unwittingly articulated an unease that had already begun to form in the minds of many ordinary Americans."[4] This unease, he believed, stemmed from the decline in the nation's social capital; Americans were becoming increasingly disengaged from their communities. By presenting ideas that were interesting to the population at large and doing it in simple, accessible prose, Putnam was able to attract a general interest audience.

Putnam's ideas have been applied to a variety of social challenges ranging from health science to the resolution of disputes. Current and former heads of state, such as Tony Blair,* Muammar Gaddafi,* George W. Bush,* and Barack Obama,* have sought Putnam's advice

and have been influenced by him. *Bowling Alone* will undoubtedly
continue to be a seminal text for years—if not decades—to come.

NOTES

1   Thomas H. Sander and Robert D. Putnam, "Still Bowling Alone?: The Post-9/11 Split," *Journal of Democracy* 21, no. 1 (2010): 11.

2   Sander and Putnam, "Still Bowling Alone?" 14.

3   Madeleine Bunting, "Capital Ideas," *The Guardian*, July 18, 2007, http://www.guardian.co.uk/society/2007/jul/18/communities.guardiansocietysupplement, accessed February 19, 2015.

4   Robert D. Putnam, *Bowling Alone: The Collapse and Revival of American Community* (New York: Simon & Schuster, 2000), 506.

GLOSSARY

GLOSSARY OF TERMS

Autocracy: system of government in which one person holds unlimited, uncontrolled power over all others of the group or state.

Baby boomers: generation of Americans born in the post-World War II era—approximately 1946 to 1964—when there was a significant and noticeable increase in the birth rate.

Bonding social capital: social capital refers to the connections between individuals, and the social networks, trust, and reciprocity that such connections involve. Bonding social capital, which Robert D. Putnam describes as tending to be inward-looking and reinforcing exclusive identities, can include, for example, ethnic organizations, church-based reading groups, and elite country clubs.

Bowling leagues: organized teams of local bowlers who meet regularly to play against one another over the course of the sport's season.

Boy Scouts of America: a popular American youth organization established in 1910. Today it has an estimated 2.7 million youth members, aided by around a million adult volunteers.

Bridging social capital: social capital refers to the connections between individuals, and the social networks, trust, and reciprocity that such connections involve. Bridging social capital, specifically, is outward-looking and encompasses people from a broad social spectrum. The Civil Rights Movement, youth service groups, and religious organizations are all examples of bridging social capital.

Circular logic: form of reasoning where the reasoner begins by assuming the truth of the argument's end point, without providing additional evidence to back up the conclusion.

Civic engagement: involvement of the citizenry in their state's political process and, more broadly, in the trends and issues likely to affect them.

Civil Rights Movement: in the United States, a movement mainly of the 1950s and 1960s. Activists and ordinary people came together to stage extensive protests against racial segregation and discrimination—particularly in the American South.

DDB Needham Life Style Study: annual survey that has been conducted in the United States since 1975. The survey contains over 500 questions on diverse activities, interests, and opinions. Putnam was particularly interested in questions such as how often respondents attended club meetings, volunteered, entertained friends at their homes, or went on picnics.

Elks: American fraternal order and social club founded in 1868 and with close to one million members today.

Ethnographer: someone who scientifically studies people and their cultures.

Horizontal networks: bringing together of groups of equal status and power, such as neighborhood associations, choral societies, and sports clubs.

Journal of Democracy: journal published by the Johns Hopkins University Press. A leading forum for scholarly analysis on democracy, it observes and critiques democracy movements worldwide, and is widely reprinted in multiple languages.

Judaism: monotheistic religion founded over 3,500 years ago in the Middle East. Today its practitioners, Jews, are largely concentrated in Israel and the United States, with smaller populations in dozens of other countries around the world.

Ku Klux Klan: white supremacist group in the United States, dating back to the 1860s. It originally directed its hatred and/or violence toward the African American population in the country, but has since broadened its focus to different ethnic minorities.

Mafia: organized crime organization operating in many countries throughout the world—notably in Italy and the United States. It is often involved in activities such as protection racketeering (providing security to businesses for a fee, often against their will and outside the force of the law).

Methodist: Christian Protestant Church founded in Great Britain in the eighteenth century by John Wesley. Its emphasis on missionary work meant that the Church expanded throughout the British Empire and the United States.

9/11 attacks: four attacks on the United States staged on September 11, 2001 and coordinated by the Islamist terrorist group al-Qaeda. The attacks resulted in almost 3,000 deaths.

Parent Teacher Association (PTAs): formal organizations consisting of parents, teachers, and other school staff, with the purpose of encouraging parental and community participation in schools. They are prominent in numerous countries globally.

Quantitative research: data-collection method used in the natural and social sciences. It involves the systematic investigation of observable phenomena through the use of statistical, mathematical, or computational techniques.

Red Cross: international humanitarian organization founded in 1863.

Saguaro Seminar: ongoing research project founded by Robert D. Putnam in 2000. Its mission is to improve social capital measurement and data and, more broadly, to consider various means to build social capital in the modern world.

Service-learning programs: initiatives that combine formal instruction with related service in the community.

Social capital: connections between individuals, and the common civic values that influence a society, and the nature, extent and impact of these.

State of the Union Address: annual speech delivered by the president of the United States to Congress, notable for, usually, discussing the condition, progress, and future trends of the country.

Vertical networks: networks that link unequal agents in a relationship of hierarchy and dependence. The Mafia is a good example of a vertical network.

Veterans of Foreign Wars: American non-profit service organization designed to provide support—both financial and non-financial—to members and veterans of the US military services.

White supremacy: type of racism where believers are convinced white people are superior to people of other racial backgrounds.

World War II (1939–45): global war that involved all of the world's great powers and numerous other countries around the globe. The war resulted in an estimated 50–85 million deaths.

PEOPLE MENTIONED IN THE TEXT

Tony Blair (b. 1953) was prime minister of the United Kingdom from 1997 to 2007.

Pierre Bourdieu (1930–2002) was a French sociologist, philosopher, and anthropologist. He was known particularly for his book *Distinction: A Social Critique of the Judgment of Taste* and more broadly for his research on power dynamics in society.

Gordon Brown (b. 1951) was prime minister of the United Kingdom from 2007 to 2010.

George W. Bush (b. 1946) was 43rd president of the United States, in office from 2001 to 2009.

Simone Chambers is a professor of political science at the University of Toronto and director of the Centre for Ethics. Her work looks at issues of democratic theory, ethics, secularism, civility, and the public sphere.

Bill Clinton (b. 1946) was 42nd president of the United States, in office from 1993 to 2001.

James Coleman (1926–95) was an American sociologist and former president of the American Sociological Association. Coleman is considered one of the first people to have used the phrase "social capital."

Lewis Feldstein was a frequent collaborator with Robert D. Putnam on publications and projects related to civic engagement in the

American community. He is co-chair of the Saguaro Seminar along with Putnam, and former president of the New Hampshire Charitable Foundation.

Muammar Gaddafi (1942–2011) was dictator of Libya from 1969 to 2011.

Maurice Gesthuizen is assistant professor in the Department of Sociology at Radboud University, Nijmegen, in the Netherlands. His research focuses on the causes and consequences of inequality in education.

Peter Geurts is associate professor of research methods and statistics at the University of Twente in the Netherlands. He focuses particularly on large-scale surveys of citizen participation in local and national communities.

Al Gore (b. 1948) was the 45th vice president of the United States from 1993 to 2001.

Mark Granovetter (b. 1943) is an American sociologist and Joan Butler Ford professor and chair of sociology at Stanford University. His primary research interests include the interaction of people, social networks, and social institutions and how these all shape one another.

L. J. Hanifan (1879–1932) was American state supervisor of schools in rural West Virginia. His 1916 paper on the importance of community involvement in schools is credited with introducing the concept of "social capital."

John F. Kennedy (1917–63) was the 35th president of the United States, in office from 1961 to 1963.

Jeffrey Kopstein is professor of political science at the University of Toronto, as well as director of the Anne Tanenbaum Centre for Jewish Studies. Kopstein's research focuses on inter-ethnic violence, the voting patterns of minority groups, and anti-liberal tendencies in civil society.

Everett Carll Ladd (1937–99) was an American political scientist who worked at the University of Connecticut. He is best known for his collection and analysis of public opinion polls.

Paul Lichterman is currently professor of sociology and religion at the University of Southern California. He is a cultural sociologist and ethnographer, studying American political and religious associations.

Glenn Loury (b. 1948) is Merton P. Stoltz professor of the social sciences and professor of economics at Brown University. He is particularly well known for his research on welfare economics, the economics of income distribution, and his controversial views on racial disparities.

William Maloney is professor of politics at Newcastle University. His current studies focus on comparative research on interest group politics in Europe.

Laura Morales is a professor in the Department of Politics and International Relations at the University of Leicester, whose research looks particularly at social capital and immigration.

Barack Obama (b. 1961): is the 44th president of the United States, serving from 2009 to the present.

Alejandro Portes is a Cuban-American sociologist and chair of the Department of Sociology at Princeton University. His research concentrates mainly on immigration to the United States.

Robert Samuelson (b. 1945) is an American journalist who has been writing about economics since 1976, most recently in a weekly column for the *Washington Post*.

Margaret Talbot has been a staff writer at the *New Yorker* since 2003, where she focuses on stories about social policy and popular culture.

Alexis de Tocqueville (1805–59) was a French political thinker and historian and is most famous for his work *Democracy in America*, which analyzes the strengths and weaknesses of the American political system of the time.

Mildred Warner is a professor in the Department of City and Regional Planning at Cornell University. Her research looks at local government service delivery and economic development.

Richard Wilkinson (b. 1943) is a British social epidemiologist and professor emeritus of social epidemiology at the University of Nottingham. His co-authored book with Kate Pickett, titled *The Spirit Level*, demonstrates the relation between equality of wealth in society and better health.

Robert Wuthnow (b. 1946) is an American sociologist who is most widely known for his work on the sociology of religion. As well as being Gerhard R. Andlinger professor of sociology and chair of the Department of Sociology at Princeton University, he is also director of Princeton's Center for the Study of Religion.

WORKS CITED

WORKS CITED

American Interest, The. "Bowling with Robert Putnam." *The American Interest* 3, no. 3 (2008). Accessed February 19, 2015. http://www.the-american-interest. com/2008/01/01/bowling-with-robert-putnam/.

Bourdieu, Pierre. "The Forms of Capital." In *Handbook of Theory and Research for the Sociology of Education*, edited by John G. Richardson. Connecticut: Greenwood Publishing Group, 1986.

Bunting, Madeleine. "Capital Ideas." *The Guardian*, July 18, 2007. Accessed February 19, 2015, http://www.guardian.co.uk/society/2007/jul/18/communities. guardiansocietysupplement.

Burke, Daniel. "Saguaro Seminar Stays with Obama." *Christianity Today*, June 12, 2009. Accessed February 19, 2015, http://www.christianitytoday.com/ ct/2009/juneweb-only/123.55.0.html?start=1.

Chambers, Simone, and Jeffrey Kopstein. "Bad Civil Society." *Political Theory* 29, no. 6 (2001): 837–65.

Clinton, William J., "State of the Union Address (January 24, 1995)." In *WEEKLY COMPILATION OF PRESIDENTIAL DOCUMENTS*, edited by National Archives.

Coleman, James S. "Social Capital in the Creation of Human Capital." *American Journal of Sociology* 94 (1988): 95–120.

Creswell, John W. *Research Design: Qualitative, Quantitative, and Mixed Methods Approaches*. Thousand Oaks, CA: Sage Publications, 2008.

C-SPAN Booknotes. "Robert Putnam: Bowling Alone." *C-SPAN Booknotes*, December 24, 2000. Accessed February 19, 2015. http://www.booknotes.org/ FullPage.aspx?SID=159499-1.

Fischer, Claude S. "Bowling Alone: What's the Score?" *Social Networks* 27, no. 2 (2005): 155–67.

Gesthuizen, Maurice, Tom Van Der Meer, and Peer Scheepers, "Ethnic Diversity and Social Capital in Europe: Tests of Putnam's Thesis in European Countries." *Scandinavian Political Studies* 32, no. 2 (2009): 121–42.

Granovetter, Mark S. "The Strength of Weak Ties." *American Journal of Sociology* 78, no. 6 (1973): 1360–80.

Grix, Jonathan. "Introducing Students to the Generic Terminology of Social Research." *Politics* 22, no. 3 (2002): 175–86.

Halpern, David. *Social Capital*. Cambridge: Polity Press, 2005.

Harvard Kennedy School. "The Saguaro Seminar." Accessed February 20, 2015. http://www.hks.harvard.edu/programs/saguaro/.

Harvard Kennedy School Insight. "Robert Putnam on Immigration and Social Cohesion," February 11, 2008. Accessed June 7, 2013. http://www.hks.harvard.edu/news-events/publications/insight/democratic/robert-putnam.

Harvard University Department of Government. "Robert Putnam." Department of Government, Harvard University. Accessed February 19, 2015. http://www.gov.harvard.edu/people/faculty/robert-putnam.

Ladd, Everett C. "The Data Just Don't Show Erosion of America's 'Social Capital'." *The Public Perspective* (June/July 1996).

Lichterman, Paul. "Social Capital or Group Style? Rescuing Tocqueville's Insights on Civic Engagement." *Theory and Society* 35, no. 5–6 (2006): 529–63.

Loury, Glenn. "A Dynamic Theory of Racial Income Differences." In *Women, Minorities and Employment Discrimination*, edited by Phyllis A. Wallace and Annette M. LaMond. Lexington, MA: Lexington Books, l976.

Maloney, William, Graham Smith, and Gerry Stoker. "Social Capital and Urban Governance: Adding a More Contextualized 'Top-Down' Perspective." *Political Studies* 48, no. 4 (2000): 802–20.

McKenzie, Kwame, Rob Whitly, and Scott Weich. "Social Capital and Mental Health." *The British Journal of Psychiatry* 181, no. 4 (2002): 280–3.

McLean, Scott L., David A. Schultz, and Manfred B. Steger, eds. *Social Capital: Critical Perspectives on Community and "Bowling Alone."* New York: New York University Press, 2002.

Portes, Alejandro. "Social Capital: Its Origins and Applications in Modern Sociology." *Annual Review of Sociology* 24 (1998): 1–24.

Putnam, Robert D. "Bowling Alone: America's Declining Social Capital." *Journal of Democracy* 6, no. 1 (1995): 65–78.

Bowling Alone: The Collapse and Revival of American Community. New York: Simon & Schuster, 2000.

Putnam, Robert D., and Lewis Feldstein. *Better Together: Restoring the American Community*. New York: Simon & Schuster, 2004.

Putnam, Robert D., Robert Leonardi, and Raffaella Nanetti. *Making Democracy Work: Civic Traditions in Modern Italy*. Princeton, NJ: Princeton University Press, 1993.

Rogers, Ben, and Emily Robinson. *The Benefits of Community Engagement: A Review of the Evidence.* London: Home Office Active Citizenship Centre, 2004.

Samuelson, Robert S. "'Bowling Alone' is Bunk." *Washington Post*, April 10, 1996.

Sander, Thomas H., and Robert D. Putnam. "Still Bowling Alone?: The Post-9/11 Split." *Journal of Democracy* 21, no. 1 (2010): 9–16.

Skoric, Marko M., Deborah Ying, and Ying Ng. "Bowling Online, Not Alone: Online Social Capital and Political Participation in Singapore." *Journal of Computer-Mediated Communication* 14, no. 2 (2009): 414–33.

Smith, Mark K. "Robert Putnam." *The Encyclopaedia of Informal Education*. Accessed February 19, 2015. http://www.infed.org/thinkers/putnam.htm.

Social Capital Blog in participation with the Saguaro Seminar. "Advances in Social Capital Measurement." Accessed March 18, 2015. https://socialcapital. wordpress.com/2008/08/07/advances-in-social-capital-measurement/.

Stolle, Dietlind, and Marc Hooghe. "Inaccurate, Exceptional, One-Sided or Irrelevant? The Debate About the Alleged Decline of Social Capital and Civic Engagement in Western Societies." *British Journal of Political Science* 35, no. 01 (2005): 149–67.

Szreter, Simon, and Michael Woolcock. "Health by Association? Social Capital, Social Theory, and the Political Economy of Public Health." *International Journal of Epidemiology* 33, no. 4 (2004): 650–67.

Talbot, Margaret. "Who Wants to Be a Legionnare?" *The New York Times*, June 25, 2000. Accessed February 19, 2015. http://www.nytimes.com/ books/00/06/25/reviews/000625.25talbott.html.

Tocqueville, Alexis de. *Democracy in America*. Garden City, NY: Doubleday, 1969.

Tolbert, Caroline J., and Ramona S. Mcneal, "Unraveling the Effects of the Internet on Political Participation?" *Political Research Quarterley* 56, no. 2 (2003): 175–85.

Uchitelle, Louis. "Lonely Bowlers, Unite: Mend the Social Fabric; a Political Scientist Renews His Alarm at the Erosion of Community Ties." *New York Times*, May 6, 2000. Accessed June 7, 2013, http://www.nytimes.com/2000/05/06/ arts/lonely-bowlers-unite-mend-social-fabric-political-scientist-renews-his-alarm. html?pagewanted=all&src=pm.

Warner, Mildred. "Building Social Capital: The Role of Local Government." *Journal of Socio-Economics* 30, no. 2 (2001): 187–92.

Wolfe, Alan. "Bowling with Others." *New York Times*, October 17, 1999. Accessed February 20, 2015. http://www.nytimes.com/books/99/10/17/ reviews/991017.17wolfet.html.

Wuthnow, Robert. "United States: Bridging the Privileged and the Marginalized?" In *Democracies in Flux: The Evolution of Social Capital in Contemporary Society*, edited by Robert D. Putnam, 59–102. New York: Oxford University Press, 2002.

THE MACAT LIBRARY
BY DISCIPLINE

AFRICANA STUDIES

Chinua Achebe's *An Image of Africa: Racism in Conrad's Heart of Darkness*
W. E. B. Du Bois's *The Souls of Black Folk*
Zora Neale Huston's *Characteristics of Negro Expression*
Martin Luther King Jr's *Why We Can't Wait*
Toni Morrison's *Playing in the Dark: Whiteness in the American Literary Imagination*

ANTHROPOLOGY

Arjun Appadurai's *Modernity at Large: Cultural Dimensions of Globalisation*
Philippe Ariès's *Centuries of Childhood*
Franz Boas's *Race, Language and Culture*
Kim Chan & Renée Mauborgne's *Blue Ocean Strategy*
Jared Diamond's *Guns, Germs & Steel: the Fate of Human Societies*
Jared Diamond's *Collapse: How Societies Choose to Fail or Survive*
E. E. Evans-Pritchard's *Witchcraft, Oracles and Magic Among the Azande*
James Ferguson's *The Anti-Politics Machine*
Clifford Geertz's *The Interpretation of Cultures*
David Graeber's *Debt: the First 5000 Years*
Karen Ho's *Liquidated: An Ethnography of Wall Street*
Geert Hofstede's *Culture's Consequences: Comparing Values, Behaviors, Institutes and Organizations across Nations*
Claude Lévi-Strauss's *Structural Anthropology*
Jay Macleod's *Ain't No Makin' It: Aspirations and Attainment in a Low-Income Neighborhood*
Saba Mahmood's *The Politics of Piety: The Islamic Revival and the Feminist Subject*
Marcel Mauss's *The Gift*

BUSINESS

Jean Lave & Etienne Wenger's *Situated Learning*
Theodore Levitt's *Marketing Myopia*
Burton G. Malkiel's *A Random Walk Down Wall Street*
Douglas McGregor's *The Human Side of Enterprise*
Michael Porter's *Competitive Strategy: Creating and Sustaining Superior Performance*
John Kotter's *Leading Change*
C. K. Prahalad & Gary Hamel's *The Core Competence of the Corporation*

CRIMINOLOGY

Michelle Alexander's *The New Jim Crow: Mass Incarceration in the Age of Colorblindness*
Michael R. Gottfredson & Travis Hirschi's *A General Theory of Crime*
Richard Herrnstein & Charles A. Murray's *The Bell Curve: Intelligence and Class Structure in American Life*
Elizabeth Loftus's *Eyewitness Testimony*
Jay Macleod's *Ain't No Makin' It: Aspirations and Attainment in a Low-Income Neighborhood*
Philip Zimbardo's *The Lucifer Effect*

ECONOMICS

Janet Abu-Lughod's *Before European Hegemony*
Ha-Joon Chang's *Kicking Away the Ladder*
David Brion Davis's *The Problem of Slavery in the Age of Revolution*
Milton Friedman's *The Role of Monetary Policy*
Milton Friedman's *Capitalism and Freedom*
David Graeber's *Debt: the First 5000 Years*
Friedrich Hayek's *The Road to Serfdom*
Karen Ho's *Liquidated: An Ethnography of Wall Street*

John Maynard Keynes's *The General Theory of Employment, Interest and Money*
Charles P. Kindleberger's *Manias, Panics and Crashes*
Robert Lucas's *Why Doesn't Capital Flow from Rich to Poor Countries?*
Burton G. Malkiel's *A Random Walk Down Wall Street*
Thomas Robert Malthus's *An Essay on the Principle of Population*
Karl Marx's *Capital*
Thomas Piketty's *Capital in the Twenty-First Century*
Amartya Sen's *Development as Freedom*
Adam Smith's *The Wealth of Nations*
Nassim Nicholas Taleb's *The Black Swan: The Impact of the Highly Improbable*
Amos Tversky's & Daniel Kahneman's *Judgment under Uncertainty: Heuristics and Biases*
Mahbub Ul Haq's *Reflections on Human Development*
Max Weber's *The Protestant Ethic and the Spirit of Capitalism*

FEMINISM AND GENDER STUDIES

Judith Butler's *Gender Trouble*
Simone De Beauvoir's *The Second Sex*
Michel Foucault's *History of Sexuality*
Betty Friedan's *The Feminine Mystique*
Saba Mahmood's *The Politics of Piety: The Islamic Revival and the Feminist Subject*
Joan Wallach Scott's *Gender and the Politics of History*
Mary Wollstonecraft's *A Vindication of the Rights of Woman*
Virginia Woolf's *A Room of One's Own*

GEOGRAPHY

The Brundtland Report's *Our Common Future*
Rachel Carson's *Silent Spring*
Charles Darwin's *On the Origin of Species*
James Ferguson's *The Anti-Politics Machine*
Jane Jacobs's *The Death and Life of Great American Cities*
James Lovelock's *Gaia: A New Look on Life on Earth*
Amartya Sen's *Development as Freedom*
Mathis Wackernagel & William Rees's *Our Ecological Footprint*

HISTORY

Janet Abu-Lughod's *Before European Hegemony*
Benedict Anderson's *Imagined Communities*
Bernard Bailyn's *The Ideological Origins of the American Revolution*
Hanna Batatu's *The Old Social Classes And The Revolutionary Movements Of Iraq*
Christopher Browning's *Ordinary Men: Reserve Police Batallion 101 and the Final Solution in Poland*
Edmund Burke's *Reflections on the Revolution in France*
William Cronon's *Nature's Metropolis: Chicago And The Great West*
Alfred W. Crosby's *The Columbian Exchange*
Hamid Dabashi's *Iran: A People Interrupted*
David Brion Davis's *The Problem of Slavery in the Age of Revolution*
Nathalie Zemon Davis's *The Return of Martin Guerre*
Jared Diamond's *Guns, Germs & Steel: the Fate of Human Societies*
Frank Dikotter's *Mao's Great Famine*
John W Dower's *War Without Mercy: Race And Power In The Pacific War*
W. E. B. Du Bois's *The Souls of Black Folk*
Richard J. Evans's *In Defence of History*
Lucien Febvre's *The Problem of Unbelief in the 16th Century*
Sheila Fitzpatrick's *Everyday Stalinism*

The Macat Library By Discipline

Eric Foner's *Reconstruction: America's Unfinished Revolution, 1863-1877*
Michel Foucault's *Discipline and Punish*
Michel Foucault's *History of Sexuality*
Francis Fukuyama's *The End of History and the Last Man*
John Lewis Gaddis's *We Now Know: Rethinking Cold War History*
Ernest Gellner's *Nations and Nationalism*
Eugene Genovese's *Roll, Jordan, Roll: The World the Slaves Made*
Carlo Ginzburg's *The Night Battles*
Daniel Goldhagen's *Hitler's Willing Executioners*
Jack Goldstone's *Revolution and Rebellion in the Early Modern World*
Antonio Gramsci's *The Prison Notebooks*
Alexander Hamilton, John Jay & James Madison's *The Federalist Papers*
Christopher Hill's *The World Turned Upside Down*
Carole Hillenbrand's *The Crusades: Islamic Perspectives*
Thomas Hobbes's *Leviathan*
Eric Hobsbawm's *The Age Of Revolution*
John A. Hobson's *Imperialism: A Study*
Albert Hourani's *History of the Arab Peoples*
Samuel P. Huntington's *The Clash of Civilizations and the Remaking of World Order*
C. L. R. James's *The Black Jacobins*
Tony Judt's *Postwar: A History of Europe Since 1945*
Ernst Kantorowicz's *The King's Two Bodies: A Study in Medieval Political Theology*
Paul Kennedy's *The Rise and Fall of the Great Powers*
Ian Kershaw's *The "Hitler Myth": Image and Reality in the Third Reich*
John Maynard Keynes's *The General Theory of Employment, Interest and Money*
Charles P. Kindleberger's *Manias, Panics and Crashes*
Martin Luther King Jr's *Why We Can't Wait*
Henry Kissinger's *World Order: Reflections on the Character of Nations and the Course of History*
Thomas Kuhn's *The Structure of Scientific Revolutions*
Georges Lefebvre's *The Coming of the French Revolution*
John Locke's *Two Treatises of Government*
Niccolò Machiavelli's *The Prince*
Thomas Robert Malthus's *An Essay on the Principle of Population*
Mahmood Mamdani's *Citizen and Subject: Contemporary Africa And The Legacy Of Late Colonialism*
Karl Marx's *Capital*
Stanley Milgram's *Obedience to Authority*
John Stuart Mill's *On Liberty*
Thomas Paine's *Common Sense*
Thomas Paine's *Rights of Man*
Geoffrey Parker's *Global Crisis: War, Climate Change and Catastrophe in the Seventeenth Century*
Jonathan Riley-Smith's *The First Crusade and the Idea of Crusading*
Jean-Jacques Rousseau's *The Social Contract*
Joan Wallach Scott's *Gender and the Politics of History*
Theda Skocpol's *States and Social Revolutions*
Adam Smith's *The Wealth of Nations*
Timothy Snyder's *Bloodlands: Europe Between Hitler and Stalin*
Sun Tzu's *The Art of War*
Keith Thomas's *Religion and the Decline of Magic*
Thucydides's *The History of the Peloponnesian War*
Frederick Jackson Turner's *The Significance of the Frontier in American History*
Odd Arne Westad's *The Global Cold War: Third World Interventions And The Making Of Our Times*

LITERATURE

Chinua Achebe's *An Image of Africa: Racism in Conrad's Heart of Darkness*
Roland Barthes's *Mythologies*
Homi K. Bhabha's *The Location of Culture*
Judith Butler's *Gender Trouble*
Simone De Beauvoir's *The Second Sex*
Ferdinand De Saussure's *Course in General Linguistics*
T. S. Eliot's *The Sacred Wood: Essays on Poetry and Criticism*
Zora Neale Huston's *Characteristics of Negro Expression*
Toni Morrison's *Playing in the Dark: Whiteness in the American Literary Imagination*
Edward Said's *Orientalism*
Gayatri Chakravorty Spivak's *Can the Subaltern Speak?*
Mary Wollstonecraft's *A Vindication of the Rights of Women*
Virginia Woolf's *A Room of One's Own*

PHILOSOPHY

Elizabeth Anscombe's *Modern Moral Philosophy*
Hannah Arendt's *The Human Condition*
Aristotle's *Metaphysics*
Aristotle's *Nicomachean Ethics*
Edmund Gettier's *Is Justified True Belief Knowledge?*
Georg Wilhelm Friedrich Hegel's *Phenomenology of Spirit*
David Hume's *Dialogues Concerning Natural Religion*
David Hume's *The Enquiry for Human Understanding*
Immanuel Kant's *Religion within the Boundaries of Mere Reason*
Immanuel Kant's *Critique of Pure Reason*
Søren Kierkegaard's *The Sickness Unto Death*
Søren Kierkegaard's *Fear and Trembling*
C. S. Lewis's *The Abolition of Man*
Alasdair MacIntyre's *After Virtue*
Marcus Aurelius's *Meditations*
Friedrich Nietzsche's *On the Genealogy of Morality*
Friedrich Nietzsche's *Beyond Good and Evil*
Plato's *Republic*
Plato's *Symposium*
Jean-Jacques Rousseau's *The Social Contract*
Gilbert Ryle's *The Concept of Mind*
Baruch Spinoza's *Ethics*
Sun Tzu's *The Art of War*
Ludwig Wittgenstein's *Philosophical Investigations*

POLITICS

Benedict Anderson's *Imagined Communities*
Aristotle's *Politics*
Bernard Bailyn's *The Ideological Origins of the American Revolution*
Edmund Burke's *Reflections on the Revolution in France*
John C. Calhoun's *A Disquisition on Government*
Ha-Joon Chang's *Kicking Away the Ladder*
Hamid Dabashi's *Iran: A People Interrupted*
Hamid Dabashi's *Theology of Discontent: The Ideological Foundation of the Islamic Revolution in Iran*
Robert Dahl's *Democracy and its Critics*
Robert Dahl's *Who Governs?*
David Brion Davis's *The Problem of Slavery in the Age of Revolution*

The Macat Library By Discipline

Alexis De Tocqueville's *Democracy in America*
James Ferguson's *The Anti-Politics Machine*
Frank Dikotter's *Mao's Great Famine*
Sheila Fitzpatrick's *Everyday Stalinism*
Eric Foner's *Reconstruction: America's Unfinished Revolution, 1863-1877*
Milton Friedman's *Capitalism and Freedom*
Francis Fukuyama's *The End of History and the Last Man*
John Lewis Gaddis's *We Now Know: Rethinking Cold War History*
Ernest Gellner's *Nations and Nationalism*
David Graeber's *Debt: the First 5000 Years*
Antonio Gramsci's *The Prison Notebooks*
Alexander Hamilton, John Jay & James Madison's *The Federalist Papers*
Friedrich Hayek's *The Road to Serfdom*
Christopher Hill's *The World Turned Upside Down*
Thomas Hobbes's *Leviathan*
John A. Hobson's *Imperialism: A Study*
Samuel P. Huntington's *The Clash of Civilizations and the Remaking of World Order*
Tony Judt's *Postwar: A History of Europe Since 1945*
David C. Kang's *China Rising: Peace, Power and Order in East Asia*
Paul Kennedy's *The Rise and Fall of Great Powers*
Robert Keohane's *After Hegemony*
Martin Luther King Jr.'s *Why We Can't Wait*
Henry Kissinger's *World Order: Reflections on the Character of Nations and the Course of History*
John Locke's *Two Treatises of Government*
Niccolò Machiavelli's *The Prince*
Thomas Robert Malthus's *An Essay on the Principle of Population*
Mahmood Mamdani's *Citizen and Subject: Contemporary Africa And The Legacy Of Late Colonialism*
Karl Marx's *Capital*
John Stuart Mill's *On Liberty*
John Stuart Mill's *Utilitarianism*
Hans Morgenthau's *Politics Among Nations*
Thomas Paine's *Common Sense*
Thomas Paine's *Rights of Man*
Thomas Piketty's *Capital in the Twenty-First Century*
Robert D. Putman's *Bowling Alone*
John Rawls's *Theory of Justice*
Jean-Jacques Rousseau's *The Social Contract*
Theda Skocpol's *States and Social Revolutions*
Adam Smith's *The Wealth of Nations*
Sun Tzu's *The Art of War*
Henry David Thoreau's *Civil Disobedience*
Thucydides's *The History of the Peloponnesian War*
Kenneth Waltz's *Theory of International Politics*
Max Weber's *Politics as a Vocation*
Odd Arne Westad's *The Global Cold War: Third World Interventions And The Making Of Our Times*

POSTCOLONIAL STUDIES

Roland Barthes's *Mythologies*
Frantz Fanon's *Black Skin, White Masks*
Homi K. Bhabha's *The Location of Culture*
Gustavo Gutiérrez's *A Theology of Liberation*
Edward Said's *Orientalism*
Gayatri Chakravorty Spivak's *Can the Subaltern Speak?*

PSYCHOLOGY

Gordon Allport's *The Nature of Prejudice*
Alan Baddeley & Graham Hitch's *Aggression: A Social Learning Analysis*
Albert Bandura's *Aggression: A Social Learning Analysis*
Leon Festinger's *A Theory of Cognitive Dissonance*
Sigmund Freud's *The Interpretation of Dreams*
Betty Friedan's *The Feminine Mystique*
Michael R. Gottfredson & Travis Hirschi's *A General Theory of Crime*
Eric Hoffer's *The True Believer: Thoughts on the Nature of Mass Movements*
William James's *Principles of Psychology*
Elizabeth Loftus's *Eyewitness Testimony*
A. H. Maslow's *A Theory of Human Motivation*
Stanley Milgram's *Obedience to Authority*
Steven Pinker's *The Better Angels of Our Nature*
Oliver Sacks's *The Man Who Mistook His Wife For a Hat*
Richard Thaler & Cass Sunstein's *Nudge: Improving Decisions About Health, Wealth and Happiness*
Amos Tversky's *Judgment under Uncertainty: Heuristics and Biases*
Philip Zimbardo's *The Lucifer Effect*

SCIENCE

Rachel Carson's *Silent Spring*
William Cronon's *Nature's Metropolis: Chicago And The Great West*
Alfred W. Crosby's *The Columbian Exchange*
Charles Darwin's *On the Origin of Species*
Richard Dawkin's *The Selfish Gene*
Thomas Kuhn's *The Structure of Scientific Revolutions*
Geoffrey Parker's *Global Crisis: War, Climate Change and Catastrophe in the Seventeenth Century*
Mathis Wackernagel & William Rees's *Our Ecological Footprint*

SOCIOLOGY

Michelle Alexander's *The New Jim Crow: Mass Incarceration in the Age of Colorblindness*
Gordon Allport's *The Nature of Prejudice*
Albert Bandura's *Aggression: A Social Learning Analysis*
Hanna Batatu's *The Old Social Classes And The Revolutionary Movements Of Iraq*
Ha-Joon Chang's *Kicking Away the Ladder*
W. E. B. Du Bois's *The Souls of Black Folk*
Émile Durkheim's *On Suicide*
Frantz Fanon's *Black Skin, White Masks*
Frantz Fanon's *The Wretched of the Earth*
Eric Foner's *Reconstruction: America's Unfinished Revolution, 1863-1877*
Eugene Genovese's *Roll, Jordan, Roll: The World the Slaves Made*
Jack Goldstone's *Revolution and Rebellion in the Early Modern World*
Antonio Gramsci's *The Prison Notebooks*
Richard Herrnstein & Charles A Murray's *The Bell Curve: Intelligence and Class Structure in American Life*
Eric Hoffer's *The True Believer: Thoughts on the Nature of Mass Movements*
Jane Jacobs's *The Death and Life of Great American Cities*
Robert Lucas's *Why Doesn't Capital Flow from Rich to Poor Countries?*
Jay Macleod's *Ain't No Makin' It: Aspirations and Attainment in a Low Income Neighborhood*
Elaine May's *Homeward Bound: American Families in the Cold War Era*
Douglas McGregor's *The Human Side of Enterprise*
C. Wright Mills's *The Sociological Imagination*

The Macat Library By Discipline

Thomas Piketty's *Capital in the Twenty-First Century*
Robert D. Putman's *Bowling Alone*
David Riesman's *The Lonely Crowd: A Study of the Changing American Character*
Edward Said's *Orientalism*
Joan Wallach Scott's *Gender and the Politics of History*
Theda Skocpol's *States and Social Revolutions*
Max Weber's *The Protestant Ethic and the Spirit of Capitalism*

THEOLOGY

Augustine's *Confessions*
Benedict's *Rule of St Benedict*
Gustavo Gutiérrez's *A Theology of Liberation*
Carole Hillenbrand's *The Crusades: Islamic Perspectives*
David Hume's *Dialogues Concerning Natural Religion*
Immanuel Kant's *Religion within the Boundaries of Mere Reason*
Ernst Kantorowicz's *The King's Two Bodies: A Study in Medieval Political Theology*
Søren Kierkegaard's *The Sickness Unto Death*
C. S. Lewis's *The Abolition of Man*
Saba Mahmood's *The Politics of Piety: The Islamic Revival and the Feminist Subject*
Baruch Spinoza's *Ethics*
Keith Thomas's *Religion and the Decline of Magic*

COMING SOON

Chris Argyris's *The Individual and the Organisation*
Seyla Benhabib's *The Rights of Others*
Walter Benjamin's *The Work Of Art in the Age of Mechanical Reproduction*
John Berger's *Ways of Seeing*
Pierre Bourdieu's *Outline of a Theory of Practice*
Mary Douglas's *Purity and Danger*
Roland Dworkin's *Taking Rights Seriously*
James G. March's *Exploration and Exploitation in Organisational Learning*
Ikujiro Nonaka's *A Dynamic Theory of Organizational Knowledge Creation*
Griselda Pollock's *Vision and Difference*
Amartya Sen's *Inequality Re-Examined*
Susan Sontag's *On Photography*
Yasser Tabbaa's *The Transformation of Islamic Art*
Ludwig von Mises's *Theory of Money and Credit*

Macat Disciplines

Access the greatest ideas and thinkers across entire disciplines, including

Postcolonial Studies

Roland Barthes's *Mythologies*
Frantz Fanon's *Black Skin, White Masks*
Homi K. Bhabha's *The Location of Culture*
Gustavo Gutiérrez's *A Theology of Liberation*
Edward Said's *Orientalism*
Gayatri Chakravorty Spivak's *Can the Subaltern Speak?*

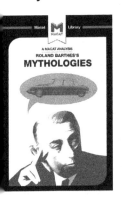

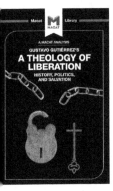
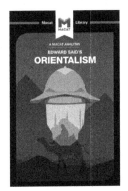

Macat analyses are available from all good bookshops and libraries.

Access hundreds of analyses through one, multimedia tool.
Join free for one month **library.macat.com**

Macat Disciplines

Access the greatest ideas and thinkers across entire disciplines, including

AFRICANA STUDIES

Chinua Achebe's *An Image of Africa: Racism in Conrad's Heart of Darkness*

W. E. B. Du Bois's *The Souls of Black Folk*

Zora Neale Hurston's *Characteristics of Negro Expression*

Martin Luther King Jr.'s *Why We Can't Wait*

Toni Morrison's *Playing in the Dark: Whiteness in the American Literary Imagination*

Macat analyses are available from all good bookshops and libraries.

Access hundreds of analyses through one, multimedia tool.
Join free for one month **library.macat.com**

Macat Disciplines

*Access the greatest ideas and thinkers
across entire disciplines, including*

FEMINISM, GENDER AND QUEER STUDIES

Simone De Beauvoir's
The Second Sex

Michel Foucault's
History of Sexuality

Betty Friedan's
The Feminine Mystique

Saba Mahmood's
*The Politics of Piety:
The Islamic Revival and
the Feminist Subject*

Joan Wallach Scott's
*Gender and the
Politics of History*

Mary Wollstonecraft's
*A Vindication of the
Rights of Woman*

Virginia Woolf's
A Room of One's Own

Judith Butler's
Gender Trouble

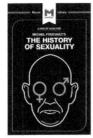

Macat analyses are available from all good bookshops and libraries.

Access hundreds of analyses through one, multimedia tool.
Join free for one month **library.macat.com**

Printed in the United States
by Baker & Taylor Publisher Services